A WISCONSIN TRA

GREAT
WISCONSIN
WALKS

45 STROLLS, RAMBLES, HIKES AND TREKS

WM. CHAD McGRATH

WISCONSIN TRAILS
Madison, Wisconsin

Library of Congress Catalog Card Number: 97-60828
ISBN: 0-915024-55-1

Editor: Elizabeth McBride
Designer: Kathie Campbell
Maps and illustrations: Pamela Harden
Cover photograph: Michael Shedlock

Printed in the United States of America by Master Litho.

Wisconsin Tales and Trails
P.O. Box 5650
Madison, WI 53705
(800) 236-8088

To walkers everywhere, especially those
of the Wisconsin Go Hiking Club,
who conduct several hikes a week, all year long.
And to all the folks who work so hard to establish
and maintain thousands of miles of trails in our state.

Location of Walks

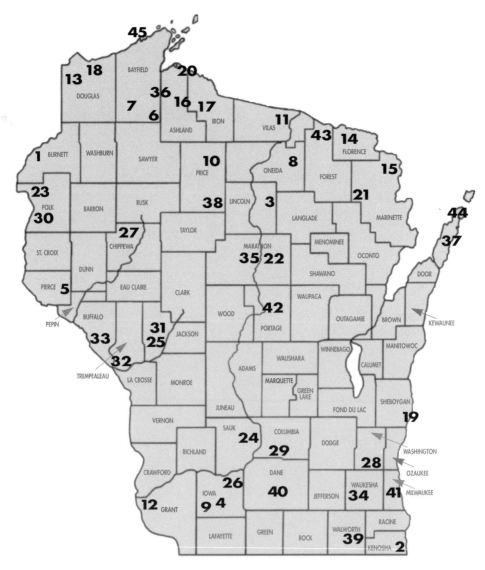

Contents

Beach Hikes

Riverside Rambles

The Glacier's Path

Walks With a View

Walks With a Goal

Urban Ambles

Snowy Adventures

Acknowledgments

Thanks to Wisconsin Go Hiking Club members Dave and Lois Lovejoy, who hiked Holy Hill with me and made suggestions about good trails; Will Sanford, who helped me with Marathon County Ice Age Trail hikes and got me connected with others who love hiking; Gary Werner, who helped me with Ice Age Trail hikes in the Dane County area. His presentation on hiking was invaluable to me early in the process of writing this book. Thanks also to Steve Sorensen, whose list of 14 trails in the far north led me to some wonderful places; Rob Speer, who led his wife Jane, Don Vogel, Paul Markovina, Liz McBride and myself on the Milwaukee Tavern Tour. Special thanks to Don for all the information he contributed about the people, places and politics of Milwaukee. Thanks to Mitch Vesaas, who led his wife Judy, Tim Yanacheck, Colleen Reinke and myself on the Madison Pub Crawl; Mary Jo Slone and Dan Slone, who hiked parts of the Ice Age Trail with me; folks at the DNR Office of Endangered Resources and at the Nature Conservancy, who shared information and ideas about places to hike; Mike Giles, Governor Knowles State Forest superintendent, who gave me his copies of the plat book pages covering the forest; Tim Yanacheck, for the back cover photo; and Liz McBride, who edits with a writer's sensibilities and coaches better than Parseghian.

Introduction

I must confess something. When I was asked to write this book, I had one major reservation: I wasn't sure I liked walking.

I had long been a cross-country skier and I'd been off-road on a mountain bike more than a few times. Of course, I'd walked before, in places like the Porcupine Mountains and the Pictured Rocks area of Upper Michigan, and farther away in Nova Scotia, Oregon, Alaska and New Mexico. But walking in Wisconsin had not been a passion of mine. About the closest I'd come to it was running on trails.

My addiction to high-impact, endorphin-stimulating exercise was pretty severe. I didn't know if walking could hold my interest, and I was pretty sure it would never give me a rush. I also wondered about where one could walk in Wisconsin; this is a nice state for sure, but not in the same league, I thought at the time, with Oregon and Alaska.

I was wrong. My first walk, on the Eau Claire Dells segment of the Ice Age Trail, found me drop-jawed at white pine trees reminiscent of the Porcupine Mountains, rock formations and crashing white water that reminded me of waterfalls north of Anchorage, and a well-maintained trail promising nearly a thousand miles of walking.

That trail not only held my interest, it thrilled me. I was hooked.

About 18 months have gone by since that first walk. I have trekked more than 350 miles and 70 trails. I've learned a lot. I've met some great people. I've concluded that while walking can be aerobic, and certainly is good exercise, it is at its best when approached as a mind as well as body experience. It is contemplative. It's a "smell the roses" activity. And the more you do it, the more you see and feel.

How does one pick 45 trails from the hundreds that crisscross Wisconsin? Well, you ask a lot of folks where they walk, then you go out and try the places they suggest. The problem is that almost all walking trails are likable. Plus, there would be no way for one or even a couple of authors to walk all the trails in the state.

So I worked at finding trails in all corners of Wisconsin. In the end, the selection was quite subjective and certainly not perfect. If your favorite trail is left out, send me a letter (c/o Great Wisconsin Walks, Wisconsin Trails, P.O. Box 5650, Madison, WI 53705) and I'll check it out for the next edition.

The difficulty of the walks described here varies greatly. Some are easy strolls on well-maintained park trails; others are tricky scrambles in remote areas. A few are snowshoe hikes on trail-less terrain and you will need a compass to navigate them. I recommend that you read a walk description all the way through before setting out so you know what you are getting into.

Also note that some walks are linear hikes, that is, they go from point to point rather than follow a loop trail. For most of them, you can simply retrace your route to return to the starting point. A few walks, however, are too long for that, and so I recommend using two cars so you can drop one off at the end of the hike and take the other to the beginning. Details are given in the text.

The primary reason there are linear hikes in this book is that our state is crossed by two exceptional, ultra-long linear trails: the North Country National Scenic Trail and the Ice Age National Scenic Trail. Both these trails are "in progress." The North Country Trail will one day be the longest footpath in the U.S.—3,200 miles long, extending from New York to North Dakota. The trail was inspired by the Wisconsin segment, and two walks in this book take you through a substantial chunk of it. The Ice Age Trail, when completed, will trace a thousand-mile path. It takes in outstanding geologic features that were sculpted by the glacier that last crept into this region. A number of walks in this book lead you to some of the most interesting segments.

Maps are included for all the trails. These maps were developed from several different sources, including official trail maps (when one existed), USGS quadrangle maps, and DNR, Forest Service and county documents. The maps included with each walk were drawn by an artist, not a cartographer. They are as accurate as we felt they needed to be to help you enjoy your walk. Note that we mapped only the trails I discuss in the text, and in some instances there are more trails at a site than we depict. If a park offers an official map, I encourage you to pick one up. These maps often show more detail and include more trails. And please drop me a note if you find errors in our maps or discover changes that need to be made.

On both the maps and in the text, distances are approximate. So is the time suggested for walking a trail, which varies greatly with the walker. Keep in mind, too, that trails vary with the season and the weather. Slippery leaves in fall can make an otherwise easy slope tough. A wet spring can shut down some trails, or at least make them difficult slogs. Bugs can impact both the duration and enjoyment of a walk. One early walk, on a section of the Ice Age Trail in Marathon

County, was a disaster for me because of deer flies. It was also fast because instead of walking I ended up running about three miles to escape the little critters.

I'm not going to spend much time telling you what you need to wear and bring on a walk. Most of that is common sense. Shoes are worth mentioning because sometimes I think we overdress our feet. While walking boots are OK, in a lot of the situations described here comfortable old running shoes will work fine. Other items worth taking: a compass, extra socks, rainwear if it looks rainy and warm clothes if it might turn cold, water and snacks. On the very long walks in wilderness areas, you might want to also bring a flashlight, matches and a first-aid kit.

Most importantly, get out and enjoy the wonderful sights, sounds, smells and even the taste of Wisconsin's great outdoors. In the right season, blueberries, strawberries or raspberries are never far away on most of these walks.

Treks Through the Woods and Meadows

1

Brandt Pines Interpretive Trail
Governor Knowles State Forest

Red pines and ferns highlight a woodland walk.

Distance: Three miles.

Time: One to two hours.

Path: A generally smooth grass or dirt path. The trail is well marked. The terrain is rolling.

Directions: From the intersection of Highway 48 and Highway 70 just south of Grantsburg, take Highway 70 west two miles to Larson Road. Turn right on Larson and go six miles to the Brandt Pines parking lot, which is on the left. A state park sticker is required.

Contact: Governor Knowles State Forest
P.O. Box 367, Grantsburg, WI 54840; (715) 463-2898.

From the parking area and signboard, take the trail that branches left. This is, perhaps, the best trail in the state if you really want to learn something about the area in which you are walking. You will encounter 17 sites with interpretive signs. By the time you finish this walk you will be able to identify half a dozen trees (including "bear trees"), four different kinds of ferns and a number of common wildflowers and birds. Site Number One greets you as you enter the woods. It tells you about the wildflowers, from early-blooming trilliums to later-blooming smooth asters.

Once into the woods, the trail splits. Stay on the Ridge Trail. Because you are on a well-drained glacial ridge, oak trees grow here; a sign on the trail will tell you more. Just before the trail reaches a crossing, you'll see lots of ferns and a nature trail sign telling you about the bracken, spinulose wood, ostrich and marsh ferns that wave at you in a "frondly" manner along the way.

Cross the Ravine Trail, and continue on the Ridge Trail. The next nature trail sign points out the ravine to the left, a ravine you will be walking through shortly.

As you walk down the trail you will see a clearing up ahead. This is an area with a shelter and fire ring. It's used by cross-country skiers, but feel free to sit down and enjoy the forest opening. If you sit quietly and long enough, deer may venture into the opening to feed on the grasses.

When you start walking again, take care to select the Ravine Trail to continue on the nature walk.

After two trail signs telling you about white and red pine, you'll need to detour off the Ravine Trail so you can find the next interpretive sign—the Brandt Pines Red Pines sign. It's about 100 yards down a hill behind the red pine interpretive sign. (A visible path leads there.) This natural stand of red pine is unique for the size of the trees and their extent. Notice the decidedly reddish hue in the bark. This is characteristic of red pine, though the color does vary somewhat with the size of the tree.

Return from your detour and continue down the Ravine Trail. It will take you downhill, into its namesake, a large ravine. The trail will get wet, and you'll encounter some bridges that have been built to span the wettest areas. The wetness is from springs or seeps along the side of the ravine. The area is full of marsh and ostrich ferns.

After a brief climb out of the ravine, you'll reach an intersection. Continue straight on the Ravine Trail. It's about .7 mile back to the parking area. The nature trail signs will tell you about several upland tree species and some of their inhabitants: birds such as brown creepers, red breasted nuthatches and evening grosbeaks. Whistle as you walk; maybe someone will answer. ▲

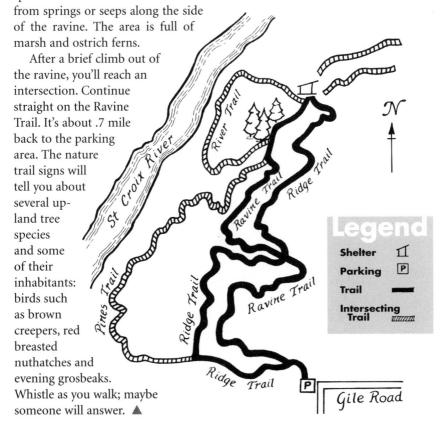

Legend

Shelter 🛖

Parking Ⓟ

Trail ▬

Intersecting Trail ▨

2

Indian Springs Trail
Petrifying Springs County Park

*Take a stroll past unusual springs and
extra-large black walnut trees.*

Distance: 1.5 miles.

Time: One hour.

Path: Dirt or mulched, and primarily flat. The trail is unmarked, except for a sign at the trailhead.

Directions: From the intersection of I-94 and County A northwest of Kenosha, take County A 4.5 miles east to the park entrance on the right.

Contact: Kenosha County Parks
P.O. Box 549, Bristol, WI 53104; (414) 653-1869.

Even though it's close to a major urban center, Petrifying Springs County Park has a nice country feel. The park takes its name from the effects of lime-saturated spring water that seeps from some hillsides. The lime coats organic objects, like fallen tree twigs, and forms a sort of plastic cast that "petrifies" the objects. On this walk through the park, you'll find the biggest black walnut trees of any walk in this book.

Start your walk at the concession stand across from the parking area .7 miles into the park from County A. Head for the bridge that spans the Pike River. The river has that milky-white look of water that's been through one too many water treatment plants, but you're not here for a swim. On the other side of the river, turn left. The trail hugs the bank for several hundred feet until it heads into a grassy clearing with picnic tables. Most of the trails in this park are like this, crossing through open glades. It's a nice design.

On the left side of the grassy area there are two trees, just at the wood's edge. Both are black walnut, each around 3 feet in diameter and perhaps more than a hundred feet tall. These are the trees that produce the black walnuts that we eat. Their wood is highly valued as lumber; trees as large as these two would fetch more than $1,000 on the stump. Here, their broad, outstretched limbs and fingerlike compound leaves provide wonderful dappled shade for the clearing.

Back in the woods, you'll come to a trail intersection. To the left is another bridge over the creek. Turn right onto this trail, which is the Indian Springs Trail. In about a hundred feet, you reach the springs. There's an old circular stone structure catching some of the water that trickles down the hillside. If you look up the hillside you may be able to see an old pipe that must have been part of an attempt to channel the spring somewhere. It's fortunate that nature covers up most of what we mortals try to do with her.

The trail curves to the right, demanding a bit of a climb. Back on level ground, near the top of the hillside, you will walk past a black walnut on the right that's 11 feet in circumference. This is very nearly the biggest in the state. There are also lots of Jack-in-the-pulpit plants on the forest floor along this section of trail.

A little past the walnut, a big boulder with a brass plaque marks the site of the first log cabin in the area, built in March 1835 by trapper Jacob Montgomery. Three very tall red oak flank the boulder. Perhaps they were there when Montgomery built his cabin; perhaps he planted them.

Continue down the path, past a big old willow tree that slants out over the trail. The creek is visible from time to time on your right, down at the bottom of the hillside. There's a vast stand of stinging nettle on the hillside also, so don't go prancing down to the creek.

When you see a park shelter on the right, you're near where

the path comes down off the hillside. Highway 31 is also apparent to your left. The hike down the hill is easy. Near the bottom there is a very notable plant on the left side of the trail: about 10 feet tall with winglike ridges all along its branches and, depending on the season, little orange turbanlike fruit hanging down from its branches. This is an eastern wahoo *(Euonymus atropurpureus)*. It's the somewhat rare native relative of the commonly used landscape shrub known as burning bush *(Euonymus alatus)*.

Once off the hillside, you will be in a grassy park area that borders the park road. Turn right and, walking along the grass or on the road, you will circle back to the parking area at the concession stand where you started. ▲

Lookout Mountain Segment
of the Ice Age
National Scenic Trail

Walk this trail in spring, when trillium, bluebead lily,
wild sarsaparilla and other wildflowers are abloom.

Distance: 3.6 miles round trip.

Time: One and a half hours.

Path: A well-trodden foot path, marked with yellow blazes on the trees. The terrain is rolling, with some steep hills.

Directions: From the intersection of Highway 17 and County B just south of Parrish, take County B west 1.1 miles to a parking lot on the left.

Contact: Ice Age Park and Trail Foundation
P.O. Box 423, Pewaukee, WI 53072; (414) 691-2776.

Even though the Ice Age Trail passes through interesting glacial topography, you're here to look at flowers. (See the Introduction for more on the Ice Age Trail.) This is an excellent walk in spring. Trilliums greet you along County B as you drive to the parking area, and they flash their white petals at you all along the trail. A stand of maidenhair fern intermixed with flowers grabs your attention about 15 minutes into your walk, and a well-drained, elevated trail keeps your feet dry even when other areas are muddy from the spring thaw. So don't let the ATV trail and well-worn path deter you; this is a good walk.

Do not start the walk on the wide ATV trail that leads from the southeast end of the parking lot. Instead, walk back to County B and head south down the road to the Ice Age Trail trailhead. On a warm mid-May afternoon, the trilliums and bird song will soothe your way along a ridge running parallel to County B for a quarter mile or so before it crosses the ATV trail a couple of times and dives southeast, away from noisy and fumy intrusions.

About 15 minutes into the walk, about 200 yards past the second ATV-trail crossing, keep an eye out for a large red oak with a yellow

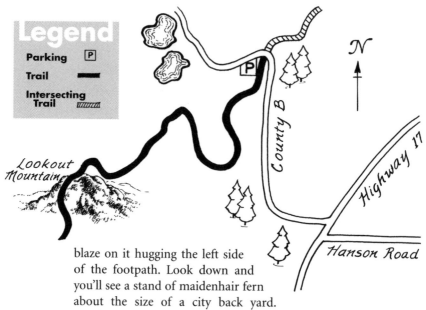

blaze on it hugging the left side of the footpath. Look down and you'll see a stand of maidenhair fern about the size of a city back yard. Maidenhair ferns hold their semicircle of leaflets on a single stalk, an incomplete pinwheel of green twirling above the forest duff. Hundreds twirl together here. Bluebead lily hold forth also, succulent-looking leaves clasping one another. The single stalk that springs from their midst will eventually bloom and ripen to a beautiful blue fruit.

You'll cross the broad and bare ATV trail yet again and begin a climb. Jack-in-the-pulpit sometimes pop up here in the middle of the trail so search the ground in front of you carefully as you walk. The hill steepens, and walking becomes difficult as you climb between red oak and sugar maple, whose fine, straight limbless trunks will make them prime candidates for the next cutting. On the forest floor beneath them, big yellow bellflowers hang off the ends of opposite-leafed stalks a few inches above the ground. Blue cohosh leaves poke their stubby, fingerlike ends above tiny grasses, and single-stalked baneberry flowers get ready to bloom. This symphony of wildflowers isn't loud, doesn't overwhelm. Look closely or you may miss even an impressive aggregation. They last only a week or two, blooming during the few weeks when the forest floor receives light. When trees leaf out and block the sun, many of these "spring ephemerals" virtually disappear until next year.

A plant that persists into the summer, wild sarsaparilla, populates the forest floor sporadically all the way to Lookout Mountain. Its leaves, tinged a lovely burgundy, are mildly hairy. Sarsaparilla stands erect, about a foot high, and always has three leafstalks with five leaves on each. The root can be used to make root beer.

When the trail takes a left turn onto a wider path, you are nearing Lookout Mountain. A real road intrudes here, along with three tall towers. The two newest are a telephone microwave relay tower and a radio repeater tower. The third, older tower, a hundred-foot-tall fire-lookout tower, looks like a dwarf next to them. A human lookout still sits in this relic each spring, usually from April through May, spying for smoke—a forest fire early-warning system unmatched by technology and resplendent with history. Not unlike the Ice Age Trail itself.

At 1,920 feet above sea level, Lookout Mountain is the highest point on the Ice Age Trail, but even when the trees are leafless the view is limited. If the hilltop was naked, it would be possible to see Rib Mountain, near Wausau, off to the south and the paper mill smokestacks in Rhinelander to the northeast.

From here, you will need to turn around and retrace your steps along the trail back to the parking lot where you started this walk. ▲

Lost Canyon, Stephens Falls and Meadow Valley Trails
Governor Dodge State Park

*A rocky canyon and waterfall are bonuses
on this walk through a wonderfully varied woods.*

Distance: 2.5 miles.

Time: One and a half to two hours.

Path: Grass and dirt, and easy to follow. The trail is well-marked and the terrain is rolling.

Directions: From the intersection of Highway 18 and Highway 23 in Dodgeville, take Highway 23 north approximately three miles to the park entrance. Follow the park road to Cox Hollow Campground. The trail begins between campsites 74 and 75. A state park sticker is required.

Contact: Governor Dodge State Park
4175 Highway 23N, Dodgeville, WI 53533; (608) 935-2315.

As you drive into Governor Dodge State Park on a late August morning, ridges layer the horizon, obscured by the late summer haze. As they recede into the distance, each ridge is slightly less distinct, but each adds a layer to the visual tapestry. There is something enthralling about this and the rasp of locust, the twitter of crickets and the chirp, chirp of robins.

Access to the Lost Canyon Trail is gained via a double-rut road that leaves the campground between sites 74 and 75. The road intersects the Meadow Valley Trail within a hundred feet. Turn left onto Meadow Valley and you'll see the sign for the Lost Canyon Trail, which heads off to the left. Follow this trail.

Soon you will enter a tunnel of trees. The trail moves slightly downhill, and several short unofficial spurs lead off to the right and a view of the treetops down in the canyon. On the slope to the right, there are some big red cedar trees. You'll pass a "Steep Downgrade, Sharp Curve" sign meant for cross-country skiers. When you reach the curve, look for some magnificent red oak on the curve's left side.

After the curve, you'll pass through a little glade, full of small black walnut trees and framed by a wall of trees on the hillside across the valley. The trailside is lush with raspberry, hazelnut and dogwood. One more downhill pitch brings you to a wet area, which, late in the summer, is full of orange jewelweed, Joe pyeweed and cheerful woodland sunflowers.

The trail crosses a little creek that at this point doesn't look like much. The creek may have a name, but neither the park map nor the *Wisconsin Atlas & Gazetteer* indicate one. When you see the falls farther down the trail, this creek will earn your respect.

From the creek bed, you'll walk up a brief grade, past a white pine that's about 9 feet in circumference. Other big pine dot the floodplain, on both sides of the trail. A giant slab of rock greets you next, the first such hunk of stone on this walk. It acts as an entrance to a gallery of big rocks. They clutter the slope up to a steep embankment on the left side of the trail.

The embankment becomes a sandstone wall, and the trail comes to within a few feet of it where it sticks out like the rounded stern of a tug boat.

When you reach a sign that directs you to Stephens Falls, take the trail indicated. The canyon walls close in on both sides. The creek bubbles its way downhill, and the path follows several wooden walkways.

Your first sense of Stephens Falls will be auditory. It sounds like someone's taking a shower, only there's no singing. Visually, the falls is impressive. Water cascades over a ledge and drops about 25 feet into a pool below. The cascade is split three-quarters of the way down by a narrow, ribbonlike beard of green moss and grass that clings to the rock.

The cascade occupies only a small section of the large concave rock face that reaches 35 feet high. The rock face looks smooth, like poured concrete, but upon close examination you'll see it is sandstone that's been weathered by smaller streams of water oozing out above and running gently down the bare rock, smoothing its surface.

The trail continues on up some steps, without which you wouldn't be able to get out of the bowl into which you have walked. There are a couple of views from the rim of the bowl of the falls and creek below. From only a few yards away, it's impossible to tell that there is a falls, let alone a canyon.

Next you will walk into a "refrigerator." The Rock Spring House sits only a hundred feet from the top of the falls. It was built into the hillside in the 1850s by Alex Stephens and his family of homesteaders. Water pours out from under the stone walls, into the structure and out the door—the same water that will cascade over the falls within a

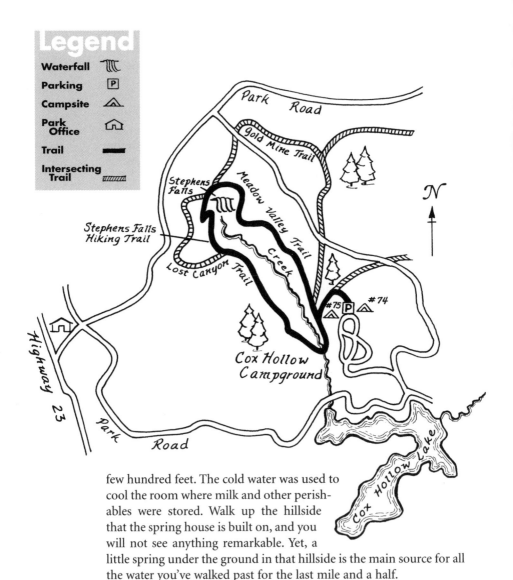

Legend

Waterfall

Parking P

Campsite

Park Office

Trail

Intersecting Trail

few hundred feet. The cold water was used to cool the room where milk and other perishables were stored. Walk up the hillside that the spring house is built on, and you will not see anything remarkable. Yet, a little spring under the ground in that hillside is the main source for all the water you've walked past for the last mile and a half.

Climb up the hill, past the spring house and a bench on the left. Lower-limbed, open-grown white pine (grown from their youth in full sunlight) and silver maple mark the old Stephens homesite. When you reach a grassy meadow and a signboard, take a sharp right and you'll be on the Meadow Valley Trail, which traces the canyon rim back to the campground.

Although this trail generally runs close to the canyon, there are only a couple of canyon views. More notable are several tree thickets through which you'll walk. First, there's a stand of prickly ash, which when covered with citrus-scented, red, BB-sized fruit in August, makes a great display. Next, after an open meadow, the trail cuts through a black locust thicket. These trees, spectacular and fragrant in June bloom, make a statement any time of year, dark trunks twisting skyward. The locust blend into elm, which soon dominate. A row of homestead pines appears on the left, not unlike the row seen earlier at the Stephens homestead. This was where another family settled back in the 1800s.

Just before you rejoin the path you started on, there's a spectacular view of the canyon to the right. A side trail is obvious, and a blue "Skiers Do Not Enter" sign warns those on slippery boards to stay away. That's because the cliff is abrupt and the approach to it slightly downhill. From the rock outcrop you can see much of the canyon below, where you have already walked. Actually you can see the tops of trees that you walked among. If it's a windy day, they will wave goodby to you.

When you rejoin the path that took you down into the canyon, turn left and follow the rutted road back into the campground. ▲

Nugget Lake Trails
Nugget Lake County Park

*Explore a county park so well-groomed
it looks like a country estate.*

Distance: Two miles.

Time: One hour.

Path: Grassy and hilly, with some steep grades. Marked for skiers, with colored markers that match the name of the trail, but it's easy to get confused at intersections.

Directions: From the intersection of Highway 10 and County CC, approximately 11 miles east of Ellsworth, take County CC north three miles to County HH. Go right (east) on County HH two miles to the park entrance, which is on the right. An entrance fee is required.

Contact: Nugget Lake County Park
RR1, Box 213B, Plum City, WI 54761; (715) 639-5611.

Nugget Lake is truly a lovely county park. It has the ambience of a private estate. The main park road back to the lake has more nicely maintained bluegrass alongside it than the Kentucky Turnpike!

Start your walk at the sign for Blue Rock Scenic Overlook, which is about in the middle of the park. Cross a little bridge over Rock Elm Creek. After a trail joins from the left, take the first right turn. About 50 feet farther, turn left. From here, you can see steps up the hillside. The first set of steps takes you to an overlook of the creek bed. More steps take you by another place where you can view the creek. After one more platform for viewing, walk south, away from the creek and onto the mowed trail, and turn right. After about 50 feet, the trail splits; take the left fork. Another 100 feet and you'll make a right turn; the corner's marked by a large sugar maple.

You'll be walking along the ridgetop, where some wildflowers are visible on the right in the less densely shaded areas. Stay on the Red Trail up and down several hills until you come to a creek crossing.

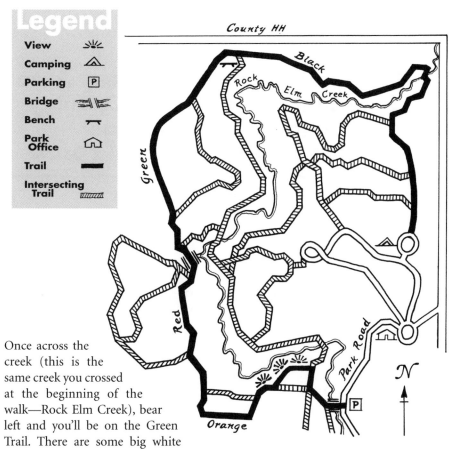

Legend

View	☀
Camping	⛺
Parking	🅿
Bridge	⟩⟨
Bench	⏗
Park Office	⌂
Trail	▬
Intersecting Trail	▨

County HH

Black

Rock   Elm   Creek

Green

Red

Park Road

Orange

N

Once across the creek (this is the same creek you crossed at the beginning of the walk—Rock Elm Creek), bear left and you'll be on the Green Trail. There are some big white oak alongside the trail here before it reaches an opening, where the trail splits. Take the left branch and you'll walk through a nice opening, full of more wildflowers. Depending on the season, you may see tall St. John's wort, black-eyed Susan, woodland sunflowers, smooth aster, blazing star and goldenrod. When you reach the pines, the other branch of the Green Trail rejoins from the right. Continue straight as the trail cuts through a dense jungle of hazelnut, grape vine, gray twig dogwood, hawthorne and pin cherry. When the Green Trail connects with the Black Trail, bear left and finish the walk on the Black Trail, walking alongside Rock Elm Creek. Note the many dead elm, both American and rock elm, all victims of Dutch elm disease.

You'll finish your walk at campsite 15 in the campground area. Follow the camp numbers as they decrease, bearing left, and you'll arrive at the main park road. Turn right onto it at the playground and your starting point is about half a mile away. ▲

Porcupine Lake Wilderness Area Segment of the North Country National Scenic Trail
Chequamegon National Forest

*Look for signs of elk on this long hike
through a remote wilderness.*

Distance: About seven miles one way.

Time: Four to five hours.

Path: Well-worn and usually dry. There is one creek crossing and one clamber across a beaver dam, either of which can leave you with wet feet. In fact, if you fall into the beaver pond on the deep side of the dam, you'll likely need to swim! Marking along the trail is sporadic, with occasional placards nailed to trees. Wood posts, with a North Country Trail logo stamped into them, near trail junctions are easy to miss. The terrain is rolling.

Directions: This is a long, linear walk, and you will need two cars if you plan to do it in one day, leaving one car at the end of your walk and driving another to the beginning. To drop off a car at trail's end, take County D about five miles south of Grand View to a parking lot on the right. To reach the trailhead from here, drive north on County D about a third of a mile to Forest Road 213. Turn left (west) on FR 213 and go 3.8 miles to the second trailhead parking area on the left.

Contact: Chequamegon National Forest, Glidden Ranger District 10650 Nyman Ave., Hayward, WI 54843; (715) 264-2511.

The wilderness aspect of this walk—no roads and no other obvious sign of human intrusion—is rare in Wisconsin and a wonderful experience. The possibility of seeing evidence of elk, or even elk themselves, is a compelling reason to walk this trail.

The Porcupine Lake Wilderness Area was designated by Congress in 1984. It includes approximately 4,450 acres of land in the Chequamegon National Forest, and the North Country National Scenic Trail cuts right through the middle of it. (See the Introduction for more on the NCT.) There are several access points; this walk starts at a trailhead parking area near the west end of Forest Road 213.

The first quarter mile or so of the walk is on a spur trail that connects with the North Country Trail. Along the spur there are several large white pine, some fallen trees across the trail and one deep, kettle hole on the left.

The spur's junction with the trail is easy to see and marked with wood posts. Bear left at the junction and it's soon obvious that this is an old logging road, the grade having been cut down on one side or the other, and sometimes on both sides. In about a hundred feet, you'll come to a small spring on the left, water seeping slowly out of the ground and down toward the trail, which is cut into the side of a ridge.

When you can see a creek down the slope to the left, you are nearing Eighteenmile Creek and Springs. Wet footing signals an imminent creek crossing. On a warm summer day, fording the creek barefoot is a temptation. If you want to keep your boots on, there are some downed trees to the left of the trail that make for a convenient bridge. Note that the creek flows from right to left, in an east-northeast direction. Unlike in most of the state, water here, north of the subcontinental divide, flows north toward Lake Superior. Eighteenmile Creek empties into the White River, which, after connecting with the Bad River, flows into Lake Superior.

After a brief climb back up a little ridge on the other side of the creek, you will see Eighteenmile Springs, which lies to the left. The trail traces the northwest side of the springs for the next 200 yards. Looking down at the water from the trail you can observe the milky, balsam-green color of the springs and fantasize about hefty brook trout rising to a spring hatch.

Near where you lose sight of the springs for the first time, the trail forks. The right fork continues your climb up onto a hillside overlooking the area. There's a nice campsite off to the right a hundred feet or so after the fork. The trail climbs some more and loops around the southwest end of the springs, which become visible again before you head up and away for the last time.

You will enter an upland area full of oak, with an occasional hemlock adding its fine-needled texture to the mix. In the fall, doll's eyes (baneberry) will gaze your way as you traverse the trail. This otherwise plain-looking plant produces white berries that have a dark, slightly elongated black spot in their middle. With several standing upright on a stout stalk, they have been named for their resemblance to the porcelain eyes used in dolls.

You will see a lake visible through the woods as you approach an arm of the wilderness area's namesake, Porcupine Lake. It will be off to your right for almost half a mile before you reach a logo-stamped post and a junction with another spur trail coming down from a parking lot on Forest Road 213. Bear right. The path brings you to views of the lake on the right and Eighteenmile Creek down the hillside to the left. The trail then leads you off the ridge to a beachfront look at the lake. The sandy lake bottom shows long, narrow, shallow striations, a sure sign that people launch and land canoes here. The beach area is backed by a 15-foot-high hillside with a path up it. Ignore this path and continue straight.

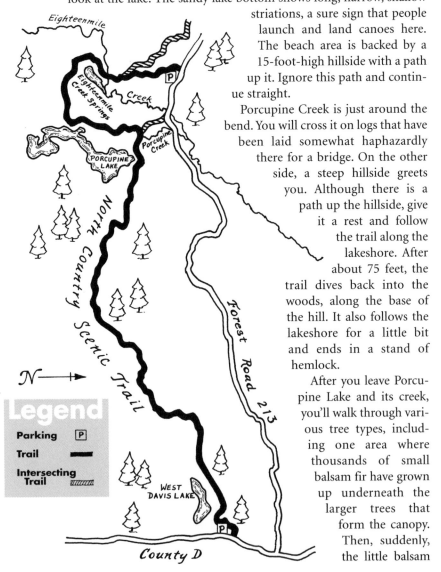

Porcupine Creek is just around the bend. You will cross it on logs that have been laid somewhat haphazardly there for a bridge. On the other side, a steep hillside greets you. Although there is a path up the hillside, give it a rest and follow the trail along the lakeshore. After about 75 feet, the trail dives back into the woods, along the base of the hill. It also follows the lakeshore for a little bit and ends in a stand of hemlock.

After you leave Porcupine Lake and its creek, you'll walk through various tree types, including one area where thousands of small balsam fir have grown up underneath the larger trees that form the canopy. Then, suddenly, the little balsam give way to little sugar maple seedlings, which form a thick carpet, albeit one raised 12 inches off the forest floor.

The trail winds through and between bogs. Beaver dams are visible in several places, and dead trees, mostly black spruce, dot the marshes that have been flooded by the chisel-toothed builders. New dams pop up all the time and you will likely see evidence of these. It's easy to tell how recently beaver dams have been built by looking at the trees that are submerged. If they are still alive, the dam is less than a year old. In a couple of spots along the trail, human builders have dug small trenches across the trail, apparently so that water will drain from one small marsh to another and not flood the trail.

It is in this boggy, beaver-pond-studded area that you have the best chance to see elk or sign of elk. In April 1995, 25 elk were released four miles south of Clam Lake by the Wisconsin Department of Natural Resources. While most remain within a couple of miles of that site, some have wandered farther away. Hikers on this section of trail have reported seeing signs of elk feeding on raspberry leaves, scrapes from hooves and horns in the sand and even hoof prints.

When you reach a colossal-sized beaver pond and dam complex you will be within a half mile of the County D parking area—the eastern end of this walk. Check out the dam. It's built up at least 5 feet above the level of the little trickle of water it dams. The beaver have used logs as large as 16 inches around to construct this edifice. Dead snags, perhaps future supports for osprey or eagle nests, stand silently in the pond the beaver have created, while ducks puddle around beneath them.

Take a deep breath and walk across the dam. It's the driest, easiest and best route to cross the wet area. From here, your walk heads up out of the lowlands into another upland woods, this one dotted with big yellow birch and some 2-foot-diameter hemlock. As you begin your trek around the never-visible West Davis Lake, note the several large kettles on the left of the trail. After traversing the wetland on the north side of West Davis Lake, you will reach the County D parking area. ▲

7

Rainbow Lake Wilderness Area Segment of the North Country National Scenic Trail
Chequamegon National Forest

Visit four wilderness lakes in an
upland forest roamed by wolves and bears.

Distance: About seven miles one way.

Time: Three to four hours.

Path: Clear, with some rocky areas and a few wet spots. There are signs at the trailheads, near the parking areas, but marking along the trail is sporadic, with occasional hiker placards nailed to trees. Wood posts, with a North Country Trail logo stamped into them, near trail junctions are easy to miss. The terrain consists of rolling glacial hills and valleys.

Directions: This is a long, linear walk and you will need two cars to complete it in one day, leaving one car at the end of the walk and driving another to the beginning. To drop one car at the end, drive to the intersection of Highway 63 and Delta-Drummond Road (Forest Road 35) just west of Drummond, then proceed 3.9 miles north to Forest Road 392. Turn left on Forest Road 392. In about three-quarters of a mile, you will come to a parking lot on the right. Leave one car there. Then continue on Forest Road 392 another three miles to Forest Road 228. Turn right on Forest Road 228 and go 4.2 miles to Forest Road 227. Turn right. The trailhead is a few hundred feet on the right, with parking on the left.

Contact: Chequamegon National Forest, Washburn Ranger District 113 S. Bayfield St., Washburn, WI 54891; (715) 373-2667.

F our wilderness lakes, nestled quietly, even secretly, in the midst of upland forest, make this walk unique. The Rainbow Lakes Wilderness Area was established in 1975, and protects 6,583 acres of northern Wisconsin forest land. Wolf stalk the area, although seeing one is uncommon. Bear roam here too, and catching a glimpse of them isn't unusual. Big trees are not the norm. The area was clear-cut in the early 1900s and periodically logged after that. Fully half of the North Country Trail is through forest in which the oldest trees are only 50 or 60 years old. (See the Introduction for more on the NCT.) Big stumps are the norm. No other walk will take you by so many of these large remnants of the former forest. A little imagination lets you see the old trees and conjure up an image of what this wilderness will look like in one or two hundred years.

This walk starts at the northwest corner of the wilderness area. The area where you enter the forest is hilly, courtesy of the last glacier. Those of you who have walked sections of the Ice Age Trail will find the terrain familiar, with lots of abrupt hills and valleys. The biggest white pine on the walk are located on the right as you hike the first quarter mile or so.

The Rust Owen Logging Company, which was based in Drummond, logged this area at the turn of the century, building a narrow-gauge railroad for its operation. The trail periodically uses the old rail bed. It's easy to see the built-up or cut-down grade as you walk. Spur lines make tangents off the main line. There are also many areas along the trail where holes have been dug for fill, the soil scooped out and put along the grade to raise and level it.

About one-third of a mile into your walk, the trail takes a 90-degree left turn and begins a long uphill climb. Look to the left as you climb. There is a deep gully, more than a hundred feet down. You are walking on a "moraine," perhaps part of the "terminal moraine," the point where the glacier stopped and deposited a pile of debris. After the trail turns back to the right, your climb continues for almost a half mile. It feels like you are headed to the top of a mountain.

The trail will have leveled off by the time you reach the first cross trail, which comes in from the right and is not noted on most maps of the area. This is an old logging road. Shortly after seeing this road, the Tower Lake Trail joins from the left. Continue straight on the North Country Trail one-third mile to Tower Lake.

As with all four lakes that you encounter on this walk, Tower Lake appears first as an opening in the forest canopy. The light streaming into the forest is a welcome invitation to quicken your gait till you reach the water. While a Department of Natural Resources publication notes that largemouth bass are "common" denizens, with both walleye and panfish "present," the Forest Service disagrees. It cites a 1984 survey that found the lake to be highly acidic, with only one species of fish, a minnow called the fine-scaled dace. Whatever, Tower Lake looks lovely from the trail.

It's only about another three-quarters of a mile to the area's namesake, Rainbow Lake. You'll approach this lake from the north and walk

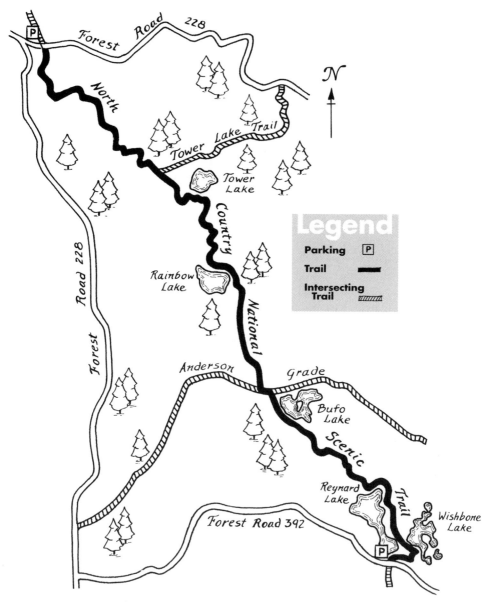

east along its northern shore for a few hundred yards. There are a couple of nice views of the lake; ducks often swim near the shore eating emergent vegetation. Rainbow, too, is fishless, save for some lowly mud minnows.

The trail loops around the east end of Rainbow Lake and heads south again. For the first time since the beginning of the walk, you'll be in a woods with some larger trees. When you encounter a cross trail from the right you have reached Anderson Grade, a path that cuts through the wilderness from east to west. Some trail maps are inaccurate in depicting this intersection and the next few hundred yards. The Anderson Grade and the North Country Trail actually join here and make a gradual turn to the left, eventually heading east through a clearing for a hundred yards or so. Then the North Country Trail splits off and heads south into the woods. You'll know you've made the correct turn if you see Bufo Lake on your left in the next quarter mile. If there's a lake on your right in about the same distance, you've made a wrong turn and gone east on the Anderson Grade.

Bufo Lake is managed by the Forest Service and contains largemouth bass and yellow perch. Just past the lake you will see some large white pines on the right. The trail here follows an old railroad grade, which ends at a wet opening. Another opening created in the canopy by a large pothole lake is visible to the south. The trail angles left and begins a long uphill climb that lasts for almost a quarter of a mile before nearing Reynard Lake. Reynard is the largest lake encountered on this walk, 33 acres big. It's 55 feet deep and harbors largemouth bass and panfish.

The trail makes its way around a bay on Reynard Lake's north end, then heads away from the lake. Twice you'll cross a canoe-hauling trail that leads to the shores of Wishbone Lake. When you reach a wet area full of alder and with steps built to keep you out of the water, you are almost finished. Your walk ends at the parking area off Forest Road 392. ▲

Raven Trail
Northern Highland-
American Legion State Forest

*Enjoy big white pine, dark hemlock groves and
a close-up view of a northern bog.*

Distance: 1.5 miles.

Time: One hour.

Path: Well-worn and hilly, with interpretive signs along the way.

Directions: From the town of Lake Tomahawk, take Highway 47 4.5 miles
north to Woodruff Road. Turn right on Woodruff Road and
go .7 miles to the parking area on the left. A trail pass is required
for those over 16 years of age.

Contact: Wisconsin Department of Natural Resources
4125 County M, Boulder Junction, WI 54512; (715) 385-2727.

B ig pine and a little bog are the two most outstanding features
of this northern trail. It's not only the circumference of the
pine that's impressive, but their height and the extensiveness
of the stand. The bog is up close and personal thanks to a boardwalk
installed by the DNR.

Begin the walk in the parking area off Woodruff Road. A signboard
marks the start of the trail. Less than 20 yards into your walk, notice
a large white pine: It is typical in size but atypical in that it has a large,
old lightning scar running down it.

When you reach the first intersection in the trail, go straight.
Continue up a gradual climb until you reach the next intersection.
This time bear left, onto the nature trail. Soon you'll be climbing the
trail's first real hill. Make sure you lift your feet high; rocks and roots
seem to stretch upward, wanting to grab the toe of your boot. There
are lots of birch stumps and logs, cut down as dead snags after suc-
cumbing to various problems that were compounded by the lack of
light caused by the ever-towering pine.

After a couple of hundred-foot-long ups and downs, you'll exit the big pine woods and enter a forest of less height and less girth. Most of the trees here are sugar maple. You'll pass a giant stump on your left. Its irregularly hollow and splintered perimeter still traces an outline bigger than any tree you've seen or will see on this walk. That's because it is a remnant of the original forest, the one that greeted timber men in the late 1800s.

Beyond the stump, you'll top a small knoll and see a nature trail sign that identifies the trees along a slope to your right. These hemlock shade out most of the light so that not even the shade-tolerant sugar maple can grow. Only a few ferns struggle in the dark. There are places where larger aspen stand tall, above thousands of small, pole-sized hemlock. Gradually these aspen will die, because of their generally shorter life span, and the hemlock will replace them as the top of the canopy.

You'll climb out of the hemlock, through small maple and into larger red oak. Oak prefer gravelly, well-drained uplands like the one you'll walk on for the next several minutes. As you begin your descent, notice how the tree type changes again, to birch and aspen, which tolerate less well-drained soil. At the bottom of the descent you'll walk through a dense stand of small balsam fir and hemlock, another of nature's dark daytime places.

In blinding contrast, the trail abruptly leaves the woods and enters an open bog on a boardwalk. The nature trail sign on the side

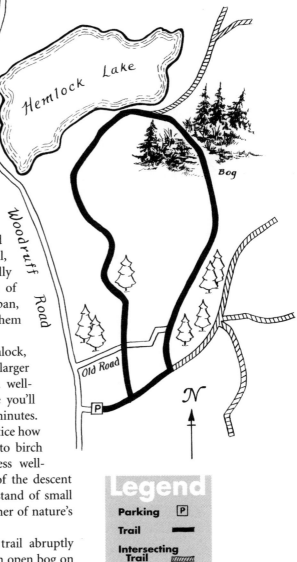

Legend

Parking	P
Trail	▬
Intersecting Trail	▨

of the boardwalk calls this a "Wet Desert," alluding to the problem the plants here have securing nutrients. The sign identifies bog rosemary, a small 6-inch-tall plant with a decidedly blue cast, and the taller, woody-stemmed Labrador tea. Also mentioned is the pitcher plant, which lurks menacingly here and there below the boardwalk. This small, 4-inch-tall plant is so named because it resembles a small pitcher. And it is menacing, if you're a fly or other insect. One of the few carnivorous plants in Wisconsin, the pitcher plant traps and digests insects to secure its nutrients.

Other plants within a couple of arms' reach of the sign include cotton grass, which stands or lies with its cotton ball-like white seed-head atop a long, slender green stem. Sphagnum moss, a main player in any northern bog, coats the ground, roots and water. Black spruce and tamarack rise from the spongy mat, their roots walking over it, digging into it, grounding it so it doesn't blow around in the wind like a gigantic inflated raft. Lily pads grow in open water, 50 feet beyond the boardwalk.

One more thing before you leave this unique, wonderful community. Notice the fragrance. It is difficult to describe. It is wet, it is spruce, it is peat. It is many things, but always the same in a bog.

Exiting the boardwalk, you will walk up a hillside that suffered a blowdown some time ago. Notice how light it is compared to other areas of the forest through which you've been walking. There's a tangle of old trees here and there on the forest floor. Once over the top of the hillside, you'll enter another dense stand of conifers. If it's a sunny day, you'll notice light up ahead, a beautiful, bright, shimmering, silvery blue hue—the light at the end of this coniferous tunnel. You're seeing Hemlock Lake, and when you arrive there you'll want to turn left. There is a map at this intersection, plus a bench that overlooks the lake.

The trail cuts through more dense hemlock, always near the lake for the next quarter of a mile. There are also a couple more benches with views of the lake. Once you trek up a small hummock and away from the lake, you'll leave the hemlock woods and re-enter the big pine. The trail crosses an old road/snowmobile trail. Stop there and look both ways, not for vehicles but up, at the great white pine reaching more than a hundred feet into the air. Enjoy the last part of your walk under these venerable trees. When you reach a junction with another trail, turn right; the parking area is about 30 feet ahead. ▲

Red Pine Trail
Blackhawk Lake Recreation Area

*Wildflowers and black walnut trees mark
this path to a sandstone mound.*

Distance: 1.5 miles.

Time: One hour.

Path: Mowed grass and dirt, and mostly flat, with a few hills. Except for the trailhead, this trail is not marked but is easy to follow.

Directions: From the little village of Cobb at the intersection of Highway 18 and Highway 80, take Highway 80 north three miles to County BH. Turn right on County BH and follow it to the park entrance. Take the park road to the campground. The trailhead is located on the west side of the road between campsites 24 and 25. There is a fee to enter the park, which is jointly owned by Iowa County and a private group.

Contact: Blackhawk Lake Recreation Area
County BH, Highland, WI 53543; (608) 623-2707.

The long downhill at the beginning of this walk lets you get your blood flowing before any strenuous exercise is required. Toward the bottom of the couple-hundred-yard descent there's a pretty view, better without leaves on the trees, of the north end of Blackhawk Lake and the wetlands around it.

When the trail levels out, you'll be walking through lush bottom-land, roofed by elm, aspen, willow and basswood, and carpeted by jewelweed, several different nettles, sunflower, thistle, fleabane and a host of other flowers, grasses and sedges, depending on the season. Narveson Creek meanders on your right until you reach a wooden bridge that crosses the 10-foot-wide stream.

The path splits on the other side of the bridge. Take the left branch, which will enable you to circle clockwise back to the bridge. Climb up into a bur oak woods, then walk through an old clearing, dotted with black walnut trees. Squirrels must have had a real "field" day burying nuts here years ago. A few large walnut trees hold sway at the edge of the clearing. It was likely their seed that the squirrels planted.

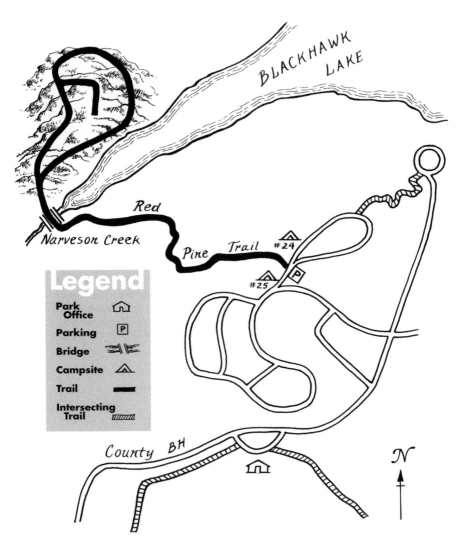

The clearing becomes a forest again as you toil your way up a steep, bare dirt path. Looking to the right, you can see an exposed sandstone cliff face. The path tops out on a little crest, descends, and brings you to a cut through a low spot in this cliff. On the right, a barely discernable trail winds 30 feet to the sandstone bluff. Follow it. The bluff isn't very tall here so look for some handholds and climb up. You'll be nose-to-frond with some polypod ferns: small, dark evergreens that make a living on seemingly bare rock.

On top of the sandstone mound, you'll see stunted red pine, short stubby trees doing their best in a tough spot. There is a modest view of the lake to the southeast, through ample leaves in summer and therefore better in leafless seasons. You'll have to bushwhack in order to explore the top of the mound. It's not that big, maybe an acre, long and narrow, dropping off precipitously in places, more gradually elsewhere. A vague, hard-to-follow game trail traces the middle of the mound to a sandstone outcrop at the other end.

Return back to the main trail the way you came: clambering down the bluff top wherever it is easiest. Return to the little crest in the trail and head downhill, through more walnut-dotted openings. You'll pass by some tree-climbing grape vines the size of a weight-lifter's forearm.

Once you complete the loop around the mound, go left over the bridge and you'll be headed back to the park road. That big downhill that was such a pleasant way to begin this walk awaits you, only this time it's a climb. ▲

10

Trail 175
Round Lake Semi-Primitive Area
Chequamegon National Forest

A gently rolling trail leads to a stand of hemlock and yellow birch, two lakes and a historic logging dam.

Distance: 4.5 miles round trip.

Time: Two to three hours.

Path: Well-maintained, easy to follow, and about as wide as a driveway. The trail is well-marked, and the terrain is gently rolling.

Directions: From the intersection of Highway 51 and Highway 70 north of downtown Minocqua, go west on Highway 70 approximately 16 miles to Forest Road 144. Turn right on FR 144 and go 2.25 miles, then bear right. After .1 mile, turn left at the Round Lake Walking and Ski Trail sign. The parking area is another .1 mile ahead.

Contact: Chequamegon National Forest, Park Falls Ranger District 1170 4th Ave. South, Park Falls, WI 54552; (715) 762-2461.

This walk takes you to an old hemlock-yellow birch stand, the headwaters of the South Fork of the Flambeau River, and a wilderness lake. You'll also see a restored logging dam. Unfortunately, the dam, which has been restored using treated lumber and modern hardware, looks more like a late 20th-century water-control structure than a late 19th-century logging dam. Perhaps it just needs to season a bit. Fifty years hence it will indeed be old.

At the trailhead, be sure to read the large picture board before you cross the South Fork of the Flambeau River. It's full of interesting tidbits of information and is accurate about where the trails go. As you cross the 30-foot-wide river on the bridge, imagine the massiveness of this same river as it courses through the Flambeau River State Forest, miles downstream. There, it's 10 times as wide with rapids that put up four-foot-high haystacks of water and souseholes that can swallow a canoe. There are boulders, too, that if plopped down in the middle of the river here would plug up the bed.

But at this spot, the river is new, having just been born a few hundred yards upstream at an outlet from Round Lake. (You'll visit the dam there later in this walk.) For now, plunge into the dense pine woods ahead and ponder its beginning. Is it natural? It almost looks that way, but most of the pines were hand planted back in the 1930s by members of the Civilian Conservation Corps. As you loop around near the shore of Round Lake, you will see some white spruce that were also planted. Spruce were chosen because they tolerate the wetter soil near the lake.

The trail crosses a little brook that drains a small wetland on the left. Then you can see a small hill to the left, "white-peppered" with birch. After walking through several stands of birch and aspen, then back into a dense pine forest (where a row of white pine next to the trail leave no doubt about human involvement in the planting), you'll come to a trail intersection. The main trail, marked 175, goes to the left. For now, bear right on "C." This trail will follow an isthmus of land between larger Round Lake on the right and a small creek, with attendant marsh on the left. You'll cross a small culvert through which the creek drains into the lake, then you'll walk over a rock spillway

created to prevent washouts of the trail during high water. The trail curves around to the right, near the lakeshore, until it comes to an old landing, which affords a nice view of the lake. Notice that the northern three-quarters of the lake look uninhabited, but the south shore is full of houses.

From here, bear left as the trail heads away from the lake up what seems to be an old railroad grade, a remnant of turn-of-the-century logging operations. The sides of the trail are sometimes more than 6 feet high. Eventually, you'll loop around to the right and enter a stand of old-growth hemlock and yellow birch. Some of the birch are almost 3 feet in diameter. The terrain also changes, becoming more rolling. Enjoy walking amid these big trees; there aren't many left. Notice that almost no little trees grow under the bigger ones. Part of the reason is that there are too many deer, which eat the little hemlock sprouts before they can grow more than a few inches tall.

When you reach the next crossroads, bear left for a side trip to Tucker Lake. It's about a quarter mile to the lake. As you get closer, you will note many windfalls, some of them big, old hemlock, and you'll have to duck under a couple before you reach the lake. The lake itself is wild, without human inhabitants.

Retrace your path back to the trail intersection and turn left to walk to another old boat landing on Round Lake. The path down to Round Lake is winding and at the next intersection diverts off to the right from the ski trail. Just before you reach the lake, there is a 4-foot-diameter white pine on the left. It has an old lightning scar, but looks healthy.

Enjoy another lake view from the landing, then for a little adventure, follow the shoreline about a quarter mile to the first landing you came to on this walk, where you can again pick up the official trail. The path along the shore is mostly deer trail, not marked and sometimes a little wet, but if you stay near the shore you can't get lost.

When you reach the other landing, turn left and you'll be walking back the way you came. In a few hundred yards the trail splits. Turn right and you'll cross a dike, climb a small hill, and join Trail 175 in a big meadow. Turn left on 175 and you'll trek back to the path that brought you out.

The logging dam is back near the parking area, on the left. There are several trails that lead to it. Its purpose in 1876 was to hold back enough water so that when its gates were opened the head of water would flush logs downstream. Water from this place flows southwest, empties into the Chippewa River, and then into the Mississippi, on its way to the Gulf of Mexico. Enjoy the connection with this wonderful river. The parking area is just a few hundred yards down the path. ▲

11

Tramper's Trail
Star Lake-Plum Lake
State Natural Area

*Yellow birch, big-toothed aspen and sugar maple
dot a peninsula that looks almost as it did
before white settlement.*

Distance: 4.5 miles.

Time: Two to three hours.

Path: A wide path, along what once was a road. The trail is not marked but is easy to follow.

Directions: From the junction of Highway 155 and County N just south of Sayner, take County N five miles north and east to the Tramper's Trail sign on the left, which marks an intersection with a dirt road. The sign and road are difficult to see, especially when approaching from the south. If you reach the East Star Lake Campground, you have gone 200 feet too far. Take the dirt road (called Hook Road, but not signed) for .7 mile to its end. You will see Star Lake on your right as you near the parking area.

Contact: Wisconsin Department of Natural Resources
4125 County M, Boulder Junction, WI 54512; (715) 385-2727.

You'll find big trees here and a forest floor so bare you'll swear someone swept it. The peninsula that is the walk's objective is one of the most relaxing places in the state.

There is no signage along the walk, save for a large State Natural Area sign in the parking lot. Take the path that crosses over a culvert—the beginning of Star Creek. Note the clarity of the water. You'll hear the gurgling of the creek for the first couple of hundred yards. Continue over the earth berm onto the trail beyond. When you reach the first fork in the trail, bear right. (The left fork leads only a hundred feet or so, then disappears.) The next few minutes you'll be walking through a variety of trees: yellow birch, white and red pine, big-toothed aspen and sugar maple. This area was logged for white pine in the 1880s, but is largely as it was before white settlement. It's

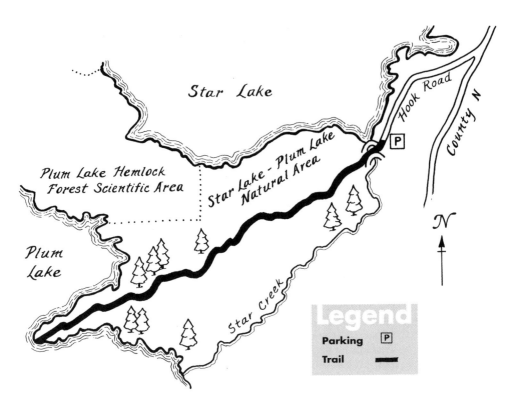

estimated that the bigger trees you are looking at originated about 1810, following a fire that swept through the area.

Soon you'll reach another fork in the path. Take the trail to the left, which leads to the peninsula. (The right path is difficult to follow and leads to a canoe landing.) On your way, look for a magnificent yellow birch on your left. Yellow birch have very textured bark, with stringy, silvery-gold tendrils clinging to the trunk. This yellow birch is about 3 feet in diameter and has a full, spreading crown. It appears to be growing out of a manmade hummock, perhaps created when the road you're walking on was built.

About 30 minutes into your walk, the woods will change. Smaller trees will predominate and the big old behemoths will be fewer and farther apart. More light will strike the forest floor and the path will get grassier. If you look through the woods to the right, you will soon see Plum Lake. It's also visible through the woods to the left. Gradually the path narrows, until balsam fir boughs touch across the trail in front of you. The path drops down to lake level.

Then you are on the peninsula. The sound of motorboats may grind in your ears, or kids playing on the beach across the lake may speak a kinder voice. Wind-ravaged red pine and white cedar cling to the sandy soil. Other trees, like birch and hemlock, try making a living on the exposed site. A fire ring of local cobblestones attests to boat landings and past picnics. Stay as long as you like. When you're ready to walk back, simply reverse your trip out. ▲

12

Wyalusing Trails
Wyalusing State Park

*Tour a gorgeous park filled with history, rich
bottomlands and an outstanding hardwood forest.*

Distance: Eight miles.

Time: Five to six hours.

Path: At Wyalusing, walking is an aerobic sport. Most of the trails are
very hilly. The paths are clearly marked but, in wet weather and
in the spring, can be muddy and slippery. The Flint Ledge and
Bluff trails present the walker with steep drop-offs only inches
from the path's edge. Acrophobics beware!

Directions: From the Highway 18/35 bridge over the Wisconsin River, go
south one mile to County C, then turn right (west) and proceed
six miles to the park entrance, which is on the right. Follow the
park road past the park office to the Point Lookout parking area.
A state park sticker is required.

Contact: Wyalusing State Park
13342 County C, Bagley, WI 53801; (608) 996-2261.

Wyalusing has it all. It combines beautiful vistas with
historic sites and places. The view of the Mississippi
from the Sentinel Ridge Trail or the view of the
Mississippi-Wisconsin River confluence from Point Lookout conjure
up images of birchbark canoes and fur traders. The Indian mounds
along the Sentinel Ridge Nature Trail Loop remind us that our history is short by archeological standards, and geology buffs read volumes
in the exposed sandstone on the bluffs. In addition, there are caves,
rock outcrops and waterfalls.

Botanically, Wyalusing is the home of one of the most outstanding
hardwood forests in the country. Rich bottomlands and windswept
ridges are full of biotic diversity. And the place is for the birds—literally. More than 190 species of birds have been sighted in the park.
Turkey buzzards and eagles soar over the bluffs, heron and geese ply
the waterways, and Ben Franklin's favorite, the American turkey,
struts his stuff.

This walk offers you a long, sweeping tour around the park. Begin on the northwest side of the park by walking from the Point Lookout parking lot to Point Lookout. The view here is magnificent. Iowa's bluffs stretch to the north. Below them, the mighty Mississippi powers its way south. Directly below, the Wisconsin River flows its final quarter mile to a mingling with the muddy giant. An expanse of backwaters worthy of the joining of these two great rivers covers the landscape. Drink in the view, then head west (left) down the Sentinel Ridge Trail. Within a hundred yards you'll see a sign directing you to Treasure Cave. Take this .2 mile side trip if you want to see the cave and if you are not afraid of heights. The cave is at the top of 24 steep wooden steps, better described as a ladder. It's an amphitheaterlike affair, 12 feet across where you step off the ladder, and about as deep. It was named Treasure Cave in the mid-1800s after local bandits hid several thousand dollars worth of gold they had stolen in it. The gold was never found, but the name stuck.

When you've finished exploring the cave, climb down the ladder and continue down the side trail. You will encounter some stairs (not ladders) and will regain the blufftop and the Sentinal Ridge Trail just east of Point Lookout.

The Sentinel Ridge Trail winds down and through an almost pure red and white oak forest for several hundred yards before a planting of white pine appears on the left. These old pines were planted in 1918 by the park's first manager, Paul Lawrence.

When you reach the top of the bluff that overlooks the Mississippi, the trail turns southward and follows the ridge until, after another shorter climb, you come upon the Green Cloud Picnic Area. It's named after a Winnebago who, in 1882, was chief of the last band of Indians to live on this land. There is also a monument dedicated to the "last Wisconsin passenger pigeon."

South of the parking area are Indian mounds and a nature trail loop, which circles them. Archeologists have identified the builders: Woodland Indians of the Effigy Mound Culture. The mounds were built between 800 and 1,300 years ago. If you want to make the nature trail loop, you'll add about a quarter mile to this walk.

The Sentinel Ridge Trail continues for about half a mile past the last mounds, descending 450 feet to river level. It ends at a road that crosses the Burlington Northern/Sante Fe Railroad track and makes a loop at a boat landing. There's a sign on the south side of the landing that lists high-water marks from floods dating back to the 1800s. You'll need to arch your neck and tilt your head backward in order to read the dates and view the marks.

From the boat landing, head back up the road and across the tracks, and you'll see a sign for the Sugar Maple Trail. To continue on this around-the-park walk, go left down this trail. It parallels the boat landing road for 500 feet or so, then turns right and begins a long climb up a draw. Depending on recent weather and the time of year, the draw may have water running down it. This is also the best place in the park for viewing spring wildflowers like shooting star and trillium. There are several places where rocks have been stacked to form a rudimentary wall, perhaps to retard trail-caused erosion.

Near the top of the climb, you will see a sign for Pictured Rock Cave. The trail to the cave is only a few hundred feet long, so take a look. More of a deep recess into the soft sandstone, the cave is semicircular and comes to a dead end that marks the end of the draw you've been walking through. Water usually drips over the edge, about 30 feet above the floor. The ice formation can be massive in spring after a winter of freezing. The cave derives its name from the colors in the sandstone. A narrow rouge red layer smears down and across the other tan layers, making playful shapes on the cave wall.

Retrace your steps to the Sugar Maple Trail, and about a thousand feet farther up you will encounter an intersection. Take the trail on the left, which leads to the Glen Homestead Picnic Area. Cross the parking area and the grassy circle in the middle of the drive and you will find two entrances to Turkey Hollow Trail. Both bring you to the same point, but take the one on the left; it's the shortest (about one mile) and avoids a walk down a power line.

The Turkey Hollow Trail is different from the other trails you've been walking, meandering through open grasslands, thickets of small trees and upland shrubs. It's no less hilly, however. This is the place to see turkeys. Keep your head up and eyes focused on distant fields. You may see some gobblers before they steal away.

You'll cross the park's entrance road, then continue north on the trail until you exit it at a small parking lot. If you've had enough walking for one day, you can walk up the entrance road to where this walk began; it's about .75 miles along the road to where you parked your car. Otherwise, take the Walnut Springs Trail east from the parking area. It begins as the Turkey Hollow Trail ended, through open grasslands. You'll cross a mountain-bike/cross-country ski trail and then begin a long descent down an old logging road. Mostly straight for its first quarter mile, the old road follows a draw and leads down to the Wisconsin River. Before you see the river, you'll make several crossings of a small streambed, cobbled on its bottom by irregularly shaped stones of all sizes. After your third crossing, you'll be in the midst of

an unusual miniforest comprised of hackberry trees. Some are quite large, more than 18 inches in diameter. Such a "pure" stand is uncommon. You'll know them by their vertically ridged or pebbled bark that, from a distance, looks like cork.

As you continue down the streambed, note that the bluff face to the southwest (on your left) rises more than a hundred feet above you. Soon the streambed widens into a large fan and the trail wanders away from the bed. Here you will see the largest organism on the entire walk—Eastern poplar. These trees love the alluvial soil here and the somewhat sheltered location. Some are more than 19 feet in circumference!

Once you see the Wisconsin River on your right, take a stroll over to it. Imagine where it starts, at Lac Vieux Desert, straddling the Wisconsin-Upper Peninsula border. The river has tumbled more than a thousand feet downhill to get to this point, near its mingling with the Mississippi. If your legs are feeling a bit tired, know that today you've logged more vertical feet—up and down—than the Wisconsin

Legend

View	☀
Parking	🅿
Picnic Area	⛱
Shelter	🏠
Park Office	🏠
Trail	▬
Intersecting Trail	▨

River descends on its entire journey!

At the sign for the Old Immigrant Trail, take a right and you'll parallel the river for a quarter mile, eventually coming to the Flint Ledge Trail. Turn left onto the Flint Ledge Trail and be ready for a climb. It's only about .1 mile to the link that sweeps upward and connects to the Bluff Trail, but it's a steep .1 mile. So is the short .1 mile link itself. If heights bother you, don't look down, just keep climbing, or crawling. Use of your hands to grab vegetation and tree stems, even hunks of mud, is recommended for balance.

When you reach the Bluff Trail, the tough climbing is over. Go left, following the signs to the Knob, which is the easternmost point of the same blufftop that Point Lookout is on. Once there, you'll see a small octagon-shaped stone shelter at the end of a road. Take the road left and in a little more than a quarter mile you'll be back at the Point Lookout parking area and the end of this walk. ▲

Waterfall Walks

13
Big Manitou Falls Trail
Pattison State Park

Listen to the Great Spirit's voice at
Wisconsin's highest cascade.

Distance: 1.5 miles.

Time: One to two hours.

Path: Stone steps, dirt and forest duff, all well-worn and obvious. The trail is not marked except for informational signs at the outset and a few other places. Part of this walk is along a geology-theme trail, which is signed with arrowheads. Expect a long and somewhat steep hill down into the river gorge below the falls.

Directions: The park entrance is located on the east side of Highway 35, about 12 miles south of Superior. A state park sticker is required.

Contact: Pattison State Park
6294 S. State Road 35, Superior, WI 54880; (715) 399-8073.

The highlight of this walk is undoubtedly Big Manitou Falls, which, at 165 feet, is the state's highest waterfall and the fourth highest waterfall east of the Rocky Mountains. The Black River begins at Black Lake, on the Wisconsin-Minnesota border and travels 22 miles before reaching the park and tumbling over the falls. The Ojibwa called these falls "Gitchee Manido," or Great Spirit. They believed that the sound of the falls was the Great Spirit's voice.

Start your walk from the nature center near the park entrance. Walk toward the tunnel under Highway 35. Before you enter the tunnel, drink in the beauty of Interfalls Lake, which lies to the south. It's an uncommonly lovely lake, with an island and shoreline blanketed by very northern-looking white pine and spruce, their spires piercing the skyline.

The tunnel is an interesting piece of work. The entrance is a semi-circular affair, lavished with stone, that would befit the entrance of a small castle. But instead of a castle, you'll pass through a 60-foot-long tube that has a top barely 6 feet high. Tall folks beware!

When you emerge from the tunnel, the trail forks. Take the right fork for now. The Big Manitou Falls is immediate, although not obvious because you're at its top. Let your eyes follow the river's course as it flows away from you. You should notice it disappear, and that beyond where it ends, the perspective changes, trees being much farther away. If you were in a canoe, this perspective change would be all you had as a clue that there was a 165-foot drop ahead! Now walk a hundred feet or so down the path to the first viewpoint on the left. The top of the falls, near where you were a minute ago, is to your left. Straight out is the middle of the falls and a little to your right is the pool at the bottom of the falls. While this is a nice view, the best viewing point is actually a little farther still down the trail, where you will find a cantilevered platform that sticks out from the cliff. The entire drop is visible from here. Across the river, cedar and pine struggle for a foothold on an almost vertical cliff.

The river forms an impressive serpentine gorge that twists off into the distance below the platform.

Back on the path, it's only about 200 more feet until you reach a chain-link fence that keeps you from proceeding any farther. There is a good view down a straight section of the river.

Head back the way you came until you reach the fork in the trail. Bear right and cross the bridge to continue the walk and see the falls from the other side of the river. A chain-link fence will be your companion along the edge of the gorge for a while. There are a couple of partially obstructed views of the falls before the path skirts the road and the County B parking area. Then the path heads back down the river, atop the gorge. You'll find three good viewpoints.

Gradually, the trail takes you away from the river, past some big red and white pine, over a little bridge spanning a usually dry creek bed and through an area cut for timber in the early 1970s. About when you can no longer hear the falls, you'll begin your descent into the gorge. It's not precipitous, just persistent. The woods become dense with balsam and spruce. Thimbleberry and wintergreen carpet the forest floor in places. A giant white pine and some wood steps signal your arrival at the river bed. The river lies about 75 feet ahead. The trail ends here, but you can follow the river up or downstream if the river isn't too full. Trout fishermen have made a few unofficial trails, but the going is rough and unmarked.

Before you turn around and return up the path you came down, look at the sandstone wall across the river. About 40 feet high, it was created millions of years ago when tiny sand grains eroded and washed off a high basalt plain to the south and settled in what was then a basin. It's difficult for us, creatures with a lifespan of less than a hundred years, to imagine the time-frame involved. Think about that as you huff and puff your way back to the road. ▲

14

La Salle Falls Trail
Florence County Forest

*A thread of tea-colored water plunges to a
wave-filled pool, far away from human intrusions.*

Distance: 2.5 miles round trip.

Time: One to two hours round trip.

Path: A worn footpath, with some rocks and roots to trip over. After an initial climb, the trail undulates gently. The walk down to the river is moderately steep. The trailhead is marked and there are a couple of signs along the way.

Directions: From Niagara, head west about 12 miles on County N through Aurora to a T intersection with County U. Turn left on County U and go a quarter mile to County C. Turn right on County C and go approximately 1.7 miles to La Salle Falls Road. Turn right on La Salle Falls Road, and proceed approximately two miles until you see the sign for the parking area.

Contact: Florence Wild Rivers Interpretive Center HC1, Box 83, Florence, WI 54121; (715) 528-5377.

This is an archetypical waterfall well worth the walk. Lots of tea-colored, tannin-rich water plunges through a narrow gap in the river, churning up an off-white foam that disappears in a big eddy-filled pool at the base of the falls. Plus, there aren't many places in Wisconsin so far from major roads that there is no manmade sound. This is one of them.

The trail makes a long, gradual ascent immediately after it leaves the parking area. Some wood steps mark the beginning of the climb. Past the steps, a big old white pine, 10 feet in circumference, greets you—a reminder of what a tree can become if not cut in its youth. In this land of little trees and constant cutting, it's amazing that it still stands.

There's still some climbing left after you pass the tree. Then you'll pass through a little tunnel of conifers, followed by a walk through a forest of aspen and birch, with a few soft maples mixed in. Unless there's snow on the ground, you will notice a carpet of bracken fern.

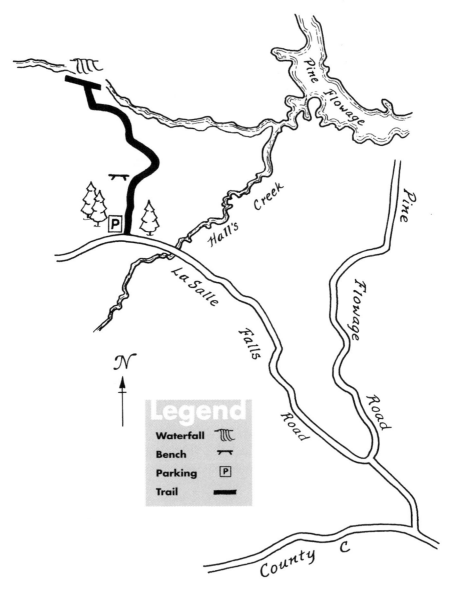

A sign tells you that it's .6 miles to the falls. A bench beckons you to sit and relax. Wait. There are several nice sitting spots at the falls, where the view is much better.

You'll walk through more aspen, birch and ferns, then cross a small trickle of water on a bridge made of hand-hewn two by fours, before you reach the next sign. One arrow points left, "To Falls," and another arrow points right, "To Gorge." Head for the falls. It's a steep but short climb up to the top of the cliff, along which the trail runs for 150 yards to the falls. There isn't much of a view here because of the trees. Keep walking along the path until it begins a descent. There are several paths leading off to the right toward the edge of the cliff. Be careful, but stroll over to the edge and find a spot through the trees that lets you see the pool at the bottom of the falls. The drop from the top of the cliff to the river is about a hundred feet. About halfway down the descent there is an opening in the trees that permits a view down the river, which is straight and full of white water.

Continue down the trail until you reach the top of the falls. There are several good places to stand (or sit). Listen to the noise the falls makes as it crashes through the rocks at your feet. If the wind is blowing from the northeast (unlikely, but possible), you'll feel the spray. Be careful, though. Standing near the falls and looking down into it will make you dizzy. (It's worse yet if you're looking through the viewfinder of a camera.) For a change of focus, look down at the bottom of the falls, where the pool swirls around in a giant eddy. If you look at the vertical rock walls around the pool, you can see 2-foot-high waves breaking on them, pretty good for a pool of water not much larger than some hot tubs.

To get back to your car, turn around and retrace your steps. On the way back, you can follow the arrow that points you down the 100-yard trek over to "The Gorge." You can't see the river any better than you already have, but there is a nice view of a sheer granite wall across the river. If you're a rock climber, you'll wish you'd brought your belay ropes. ▲

15

Long Slide Falls Trail
Long Slide Falls County Park

*A short walk, with some tricky footwork,
is rewarded by a tall cascade.*

Distance: One mile round trip.

Time: 30 to 60 minutes.

Path: The trailhead is marked. There are no other signs along the trail,
but the footpath—on dirt, rock fragments and boulders—is worn
and easy to follow. The terrain is essentially flat up to the falls
overlook; the last 200 feet require a little fancy footwork over
uneven hunks of rock. Viewing the falls from below involves a
hike down the ridge to the riverbed.

Directions: From Pembine go north on Highway 8 approximately 6.5 miles
to Morgan Park Road. Go right on Morgan Park 2.5 miles to the
parking lot entrance on the right.

Contact: Marinette Chamber of Commerce
Box 512, 601 Marinette Ave., Marinette, WI 54143; (800) 236-6681.

The walk to the top of this remote, impressive, 50-foot cascade is
one of the easiest in this book. But it isn't boring. A sign at the
beginning of the path says, "Warning: Dangerous Overlook. Parents should accompany children." A greeting like that, plus the roar of
the falls, raises your expectations as you walk the flat, level path.

You're going to walk to the top of the falls first. So bear right whenever there's a junction with another trail. You will reach the very top
of Long Slide Falls about 400 yards from the warning sign. If you then
walk downriver along the granite outcrops, you'll come to an even
better view of the falls. Here you will want to look upriver, around the
apex of the little bend that you stand on. As far as you can see, the
river is a placid, 40-foot-wide stream. Tree limbs from opposite sides
of the river form a canopy. Imagine canoeing peacefully down this
stretch, perhaps gnawing on a hunk of cheese, sipping a beer, paddle
laid lazily across the gunnels. Your canoe slips around the little bend,
and suddenly you hear the roar, as your bow dips down into the first
10-foot drop. Too late. You're in for a "long slide."

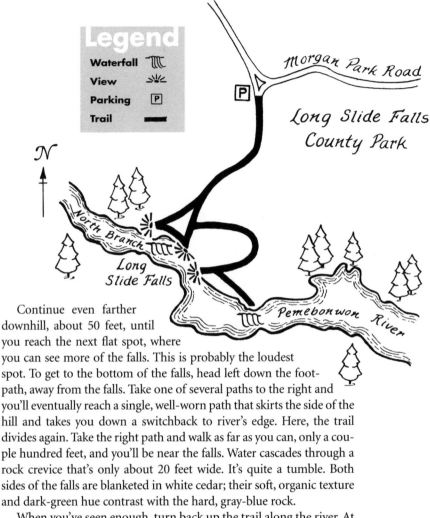

Continue even farther downhill, about 50 feet, until you reach the next flat spot, where you can see more of the falls. This is probably the loudest spot. To get to the bottom of the falls, head left down the footpath, away from the falls. Take one of several paths to the right and you'll eventually reach a single, well-worn path that skirts the side of the hill and takes you down a switchback to river's edge. Here, the trail divides again. Take the right path and walk as far as you can, only a couple hundred feet, and you'll be near the falls. Water cascades through a rock crevice that's only about 20 feet wide. It's quite a tumble. Both sides of the falls are blanketed in white cedar; their soft, organic texture and dark-green hue contrast with the hard, gray-blue rock.

When you've seen enough, turn back up the trail along the river. At the juncture where you came down off the hillside, go straight along the river. After hiking about a quarter-mile through some alder and evergreens, you'll emerge on a point of land that juts out into the river, pinching it into another small falls. Although the trail continues downstream for another few hundred feet, it ends in a tangle of alder and prickly ash.

On your way back, before you reach the juncture where you'll turn right and climb back up the hillside, there's a nice view (especially when leaves are off the trees) of the sheer granite wall that forms the escarpment from which the river drops.

The climb back up the hillside is steep, but take heart, it's also short. ▲

16

Nature and Bluestone Falls Trails
Copper Falls State Park

An up-and-down path leads to two crashing waterfalls.

Distance: 2.3 miles.

Time: One and a half hours.

Path: Generally a dirt- and duff-covered affair, punctuated by steps of beautiful black granite rock, over hilly terrain. There is one demanding climb. The route is well-marked and signed with informational placards.

Directions: From the junction of Highway 13 and Highway 169 just north of Mellen, take 169 north three miles to the park entrance on the left. Follow the park road to its end at the concession stand and picnic grounds. A state park sticker is required.

Contact: Copper Falls State Park
P.O. Box 17AA, Mellen, WI 54546; (715) 274-5123.

Start your walk at the first bridge over the Bad River. On your way notice the stone path. It's constructed of a locally quarried slate. Also note the steps to and from the bridge; they were built in the early 1930s by the Civilian Conservation Corps from black gabbro, locally called black granite. The latter rock is found in only two regions in the world, around Mellen and in the Swiss Alps.

The other impressive feature at the outset of this walk is the bridge itself. Constructed of wood, it is massive and architecturally appealing. Once across the bridge, climb the stone steps and take the first left turn in the trail. Be prepared for more climbing. There are 15 sets of stairs up the hillside. Once you are up them, the path traces the top of a bluff that overlooks the river on the left. There are three side paths you can take that lead out to the edge and a bit of a view. The best view, however, is 75 more stair steps away, at the top of an observation tower.

From the tower, looking north you can see a slice of Lake Superior and the bluffs of the Bayfield Peninsula beyond. To the south, the hills of the Penokee Range stretch from left to right. Mt. Whittlesey, topped by a tower, sticks up above all else in the southeast.

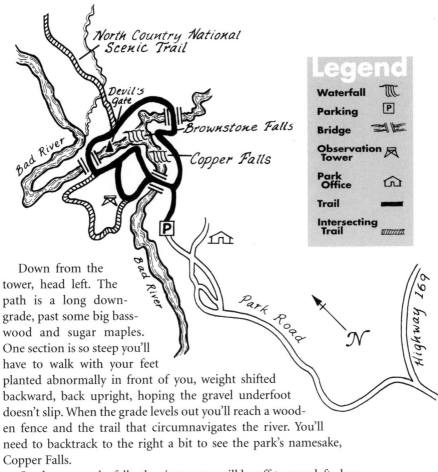

Legend

Waterfall	〽
Parking	P
Bridge	⊒‖⊑
Observation Tower	𝍓
Park Office	⌂
Trail	▬
Intersecting Trail	▨

Down from the tower, head left. The path is a long down-grade, past some big basswood and sugar maples. One section is so steep you'll have to walk with your feet planted abnormally in front of you, weight shifted backward, back upright, hoping the gravel underfoot doesn't slip. When the grade levels out you'll reach a wooden fence and the trail that circumnavigates the river. You'll need to backtrack to the right a bit to see the park's namesake, Copper Falls.

On the way to the falls, the river gorge will be off to your left, deep but hidden by trees. Just before reaching the falls, you'll begin to see through the vegetation and appreciate the depth of the gorge.

The placard at Copper Falls viewpoint tells you about the falls. Most surprisingly, the falls is eroding, its vertical drop decreasing. There are some pictures back in the park office taken in 1904 that clearly show a higher falls. The falls is becoming a rapids, water bubbling down over chunks of rock ripped from a precipice by years of hydraulic pressure and periodic freezing.

After viewing the falls, turn around and head back down the trail you just walked here on, with Brownstone Falls your next goal. There are several places along the way where you can view the river gorge and stands of white cedar, their new, light-green needles and older, richer, dark-green needles forming two-tone, frondlike fans that catch every bit of sunlight they can.

Your first view of Brownstone Falls comes at a 90-degree angle in the river and the trail. Brownstone Falls, on Tyler's Forks Creek, is more impressive than Copper Falls. With about 30 feet of vertical drop, mostly all at once rather than stretched out along the river bed, Brownstone crashes. You'll get several more good views of Brownstone after you cross the river and walk along the opposite branch.

Continue walking down the trail, past a particularly large white pine with a double leader, and you'll reach a spot where the river pinches through what's called Devil's Gate. This is a narrow place in the river created when the water eroded a conglomerate rock more quickly than the surrounding bedrock. Then walk past a covered wooden bench, through a lovely little wooded glen and down masterfully sculpted black slate stairs to a steel and wood bridge that crosses the Bad River. Look upriver for a good view of Devil's Gate.

After crossing the river, there are a couple of sets of stairs that take you to an overlook on top of Devil's Gate. Then you'll reach an intersection with the North Country Trail. If you make a left turn, you'll head downriver where there are some backpacking campsites. To continue this walk, turn right.

The next viewpoint is down some stairs to the right. Here a deck overlooks the cascades on Tyler's Forks, where water boils over several ledges. Cross the bridge beyond to arrive at one more deck. This one gives you a good, close-up view of Brownstone Falls and the Bad River below. Note how narrow the river gorge is just below the falls.

From this point it's a short quarter-mile back to the parking area. Just before you arrive there, you'll pass a sandy spit of land that juts out into the river. Look out over the water. You are seeing the placid pool that sits atop Copper Falls. There's little hint of the crashing, turbulent water just 50 yards from you.

The trail will take you back by the first bridge you crossed and then to the parking area. ▲

17
Potato River Falls Trail
Gurney Town Park

A short walk, or a longer scramble,
takes you to a series of waterfalls that
thunder through an impressive gorge.

Distance: 1.5 miles.

Time: One to two hours.

Path: The path to the overlook is well-worn and easy to follow. There are various other paths that have been worn into the hillside that overlooks the falls. These all funnel into one path that drops down the hillside to the river. The walking here is not easy; the slope is steep and will be slippery if the soil is wet from rain or melting snow.

Directions: From the intersection of Highway 2 and Highway 169, about 15 miles east of Hurley, take Highway 169 south 2.8 miles to Potato River Falls Road. Turn right and drive 1.5 miles to the town park and a small parking area. The footpath to the overview of the falls is located at the northwest corner of the parking area.

Contact: Iron County Development Zone
P.O. Box 97-WT, Hurley, WI 54543; (715) 561-2922.

There are no geometric rules defining "waterfalls." Many of Wisconsin's falls seem more like glorified rapids, with horizontal runs that roughly equal their vertical drops. The Potato River Falls, on the other hand, is a series of falls that all involve a precipitous drop. And if these falls aren't impressive enough, their deep gorge setting should be.

From the unimproved parking and camping area there are a couple of paths leading to views of the falls. Find the path that leads from the northwest corner of the parking lot toward the river gorge. After a short hundred-foot walk, you'll come to an overlook. The falls you see off to your left is only one of five that make up the Potato River Falls. From this distance, the gorge below and off to the right is as impressive as the falls. The view is Western: big, expansive.

To see the rest of the falls complex, walk to the left, upriver from

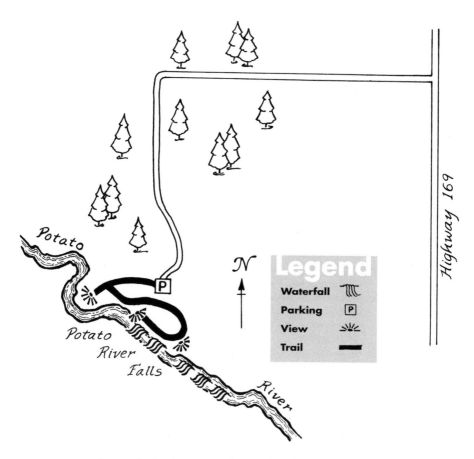

Legend

Waterfall
Parking
View
Trail

N

Potato

P

Potato River Falls

River

Highway 169

the overlook, along one of several trails that hug the top of the steep cliff. You'll cross two places where the trail has washed out, sending tons of soil and rock, plus a few trees, down the hillside and into the river. Be careful.

Eventually, the path will lead downward. An attempt has been made to construct steps in the hillside path. They are not in good shape, but if you persevere, you'll arrive at a series of overlooks. Follow the path downstream and you will see more and more waterfalls. (The path is eroded, brushy and a little dangerous—the parks people plan to improve it.) The fourth falls are broad, stretching across the entire bottom of the gorge.

After about 75 feet of walking, you'll come to the last and biggest falls of the Potato River Falls complex. You'll look down on a raging white torrent as it drops over a precipice and crashes onto rocks 45 feet below. Just above the falls is a small island, where young cedar, birch and pine hold on for dear life. Perhaps that island, those trees or their predecessors have saved a life or two, providing landfall to surprised canoeists or crazy kayakers. From your elevated perch, you can see across the gorge, where cedar, hemlock and pine vie for sunlight and hide the sheer rock face behind them. Ninety-foot-tall treetops wave in the breeze below you.

If you want to continue, the path leads down the steep slope to the riverbank just below the big falls. The spray will get you wet on a good day. Look back up at the falls from a gravel bar or rock perch a few yards out in the river. You can see the river's handiwork, the carving it's done over the last 10,000 or so years, shooting through a rock wall that's been worn down 30 feet from the surrounding cliff. Drink in the bright light reflected off foaming water, and enjoy the roar of one of Wisconsin's neatest waterfalls.

Retrace your steps to get back to your starting point. ▲

18

Waterfalls Trail
Amnicon Falls State Park

*A series of scenic waterfalls tumble
alongside a short riverside path.*

Distance: One-half mile.

Time: One hour.

Path: The trail is occasionally marked and is easy to follow since it is bounded by the river. Sites of interest are marked with an arrowhead sign. The terrain contains some small hills and climbs.

Directions: From the intersection of Highway 2 and Highway 53 southeast of Superior, go east one mile on Highway 2. Turn left on County U. The park entrance is on the left. A state park sticker is required.

Contact: Amnicon Falls State Park
6294 S. State Road 35, Superior, WI 54880; (715) 399-8073.

Amnicon is perhaps the only state park in Wisconsin where you hear the sound of falling water as you exit your car. Alongside the parking area, the Amnicon River rushes down to Lake Superior over a 4-foot falls. The sound whets your appetite for a walk that will let you hear more, along a short stretch of river packed with tumbling water.

Pick up the intelligent and easy-to-understand geology booklet available at the park office. Then begin walking just upriver from the covered bridge that is visible from the parking area. At Arrowhead One you will get a view of the Upper Falls, the biggest of the falls at Amnicon. The type of rock it flows over is called basalt, which is one-billion-year-old solidified lava.

Walk downstream about 75 feet, past the bridge, and look back upriver. From here you can see the Lower Falls. These falls tumble over sandstone, not basalt. Look around you and you can see more of this reddish sandstone, which will look familiar if you have hiked the shoreline around the Apostle Islands.

Follow the trail back upstream to the bridge and head across it, stopping to view both the Upper and Lower Falls. Note the bridge

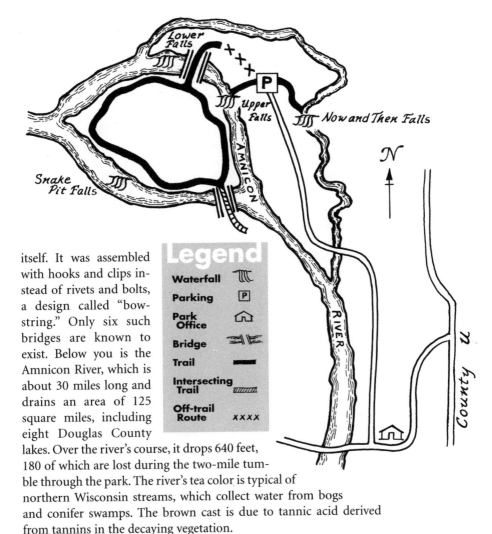

Legend

Waterfall	≈
Parking	P
Park Office	⌂
Bridge	⧫
Trail	▬
Intersecting Trail	░
Off-trail Route	xxxx

itself. It was assembled with hooks and clips instead of rivets and bolts, a design called "bowstring." Only six such bridges are known to exist. Below you is the Amnicon River, which is about 30 miles long and drains an area of 125 square miles, including eight Douglas County lakes. Over the river's course, it drops 640 feet, 180 of which are lost during the two-mile tumble through the park. The river's tea color is typical of northern Wisconsin streams, which collect water from bogs and conifer swamps. The brown cast is due to tannic acid derived from tannins in the decaying vegetation.

Once across the bridge, bear left and find Arrowhead Three near a bench along the top of a little cliff overlooking the river. Besides nice views upstream and down of Upper and Lower Falls, you can see here the park's outstanding geological feature: the "Douglas Fault." Running from near the Twin Cities in Minnesota to east of Ashland, Wisconsin, the Douglas Fault marks a 500-million-year-old fracturing of bedrock basalt. This bedrock rose upwards, perhaps three miles. The sandstone that had been on top of this bedrock eroded away. The sandstone north of the fault, which did not rise up, did not erode as much and is still visible. Look to the front of and behind the stairway that comes down off the pathway on the other side of the river. You can see today's transition zone where basalt and sandstone meet. On the upstream side of the zone, notice the different angle of the rocks. These are basalt, which were thrust upward at the fault site and angled 50 to 60 degrees. Downstream, the neatly layered sandstone lies undisturbed. In the transition zone in between, the sandstone is poorly defined and swirled, with pieces of basalt mixed in.

Continue walking upstream through the pines along the river. When you reach Arrowhead Four, take a little walk out onto the river rocks. (If they are visible. When the river is high they will be submerged.) A 6-foot-high falls down a little chute begs to be jumped, but don't try—it's a bit too wide. You can gain a more reasonable thrill by sitting down on one of the midriver rocks and looking upstream. Because you're sitting low, you'll think you're going to get wet, but you won't—the water follows the little chute.

Back on the path, continue upstream to a bridge. Turn right at the bridge and follow the west branch of the river downstream to Arrowhead Five. There are big blocks of basalt rock here, between you and the river. By closely examining the rocks, you can discern different lava flows, which are slightly different colors. The river in front of you falls over an 8-foot-high ledge formed by one of these lava flows.

Now it's time to view Snake Pit Falls. It's near Arrowhead Six. Be careful when you reach it; the edge of the cliff is unguarded, and, while the drop is only about 30 feet, it would be painful to tumble down. Snake Pit Falls has three pitches. The first is a 30-foot drop down an eroded basalt ledge onto another ledge. From there the river drops eight more feet, then twists 100 degrees before dropping another 10 feet or so.

Past Snake Pit Falls you'll walk along a ravine on the left. The river here has cut the ravine along the Douglas Fault, in an area where the rock offered less resistance than the solid basalt on which you're walking. You'll approach the main river channel and curve right, keeping the river on your left. Walk up the small hill, past Lower Falls and cross back over the river on the covered bridge.

Climb down the stairs you viewed from the other side of the river earlier for an intimate view of the Douglas Fault. Close up and personal, the fault is easy to see. If you'd like to see one more falls, cross the parking lot and walk the 20-foot path into the woods to view Now and Then Falls. ▲

Beach
Hikes

19

Kohler Dunes Cordwalk and Creeping Juniper Nature Trail
Kohler-Andrae State Parks

Experience Florida in Wisconsin—
inviting sand dunes and maritime smells.

Distance: 2.5 miles.

Time: One and a half to two and a half hours; more if you explore the beach.

Path: The cordwalk is a manmade walkway of boards strung together with rope and laid on the ground. Well-marked, it provides a visible, solid path through an ever-changing desert of sand.

Directions: From the intersection of I-43 and County V just south of Sheboygan, take County V one mile east to County KK. Turn right on County KK and go south one mile to the T intersection with Old Park Road. Turn left on Old Park Road and you will enter the park. A state park sticker is required.

Contact: Kohler-Andrae State Parks
1520 Old Park Road, Sheboygan, WI 53081; (414) 451-4080.

This is Florida in Wisconsin. On a warm summer's day you expect to taste salt in the water, or see a brown pelican scoop up a mackerel. The dunes are austere but wonderful, full of unsuspected life. By midsummer, the water's warm and inviting. It's a difficult place from which to pull yourself away.

Start this walk at the Sanderling Nature Center with a short excursion east from the parking lot, around the center and out onto the cordwalk. This takes you up a little dune and out onto the beach. The sand next to the cordwalk is so deep, so loose, so wonderfully windblown and drifted that your feet would slip if you tried to walk on it. Once you top the little dune that is the 100-year high-water mark, the lake fills your senses. If it's a warm, bright July day, with just a bit of onshore breeze, you'll smell the wet, maritime fragrance that is big water. You'll hear the gentle slosh as small waves wash over the sand. You'll see the vast expanse of blue-green lake that stretches out of sight to an ambiguous joining with the sky.

While it's tempting to end the walk before it begins and plop down right here on the beach, let's continue. Backtrack to the parking lot; the .6-mile Creeping Juniper Nature Trail loop starts at the south end. The cordwalk path traces a trail for about 200 yards along the edge of the beach, where beach grass has stabilized the dunes. You'll approach a small grove of cedar. They create a little grotto near the beach, where their shade and stabilizing roots have sheltered other plants, especially creeping juniper.

From this grotto, the trail angles away from the beach and up into the dunes. You'll reach a junction where you may go straight or right. This spot is on top of one of the higher dunes and the view is good. Beyond the dunes to the west are the forested sloughs of the Black River. Turn right to stay on the nature trail.

Walking west, you'll cross a series of dunes, each a bit smaller than the one before. In some of the bowls between dune crests the cordwalk is buried by sand. Eventually, dune grass becomes evident on the dunes. Milkweed plants seem to favor the cordwalk path itself and grow through and around it in great profusion. It's difficult to believe that this land, these piles of sand, were farmed back in the 1920s and 30s, but you can see the large Scotch pine that were planted back then as a windbreak. Park officials are gradually removing the Scotch pine so they don't colonize the dunes, thereby changing the nature of the place. The trail makes a semicircle around the rows of pine, but before they block your view of where you've walked from, look back. From this vantage point, you can appreciate the height of the dunes looming over the lake. Let your gaze trace the grass-tufted dune-tops as they paint a fuzzy, irregular, mounded line across the horizon.

A nature trail sign will point out a stand of dune thistle and thick-spike wheatgrass, both rare plants. Blazing star briefly replaces milkweed as the predominant plant near the cordwalk. The trail will exit the dunes and deliver you back to the nature center parking lot.

Continue the walk by crossing the road where it widens into the parking lot. The Kohler Dunes Cordwalk starts just off the road. After about 150 feet, the cordwalk separates into two paths. Take the one on the right. You can see a bench up a dune on the lake side. Walk to the bench and have a seat. The bench affords you a commanding view of the lake. There's always something going on out there. Fishing boats troll the waters for salmon and trout, gulls bob up and down or fly around looking for something, perhaps each other. You can see the beach's first barrier dune undulate away to the north until your view is blocked by a tall dune. Trees hug the unseen beach beyond and

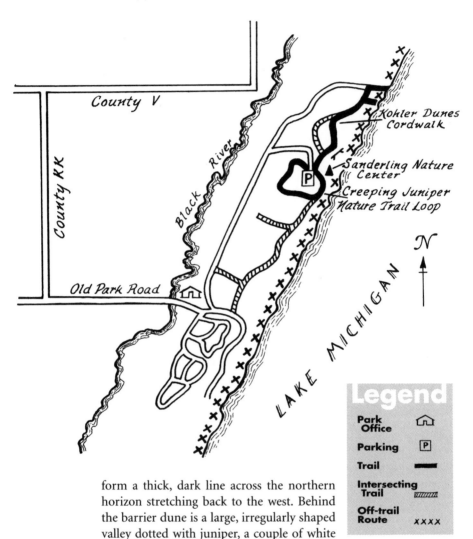

County V

County KK

Black River

Kohler Dunes Cordwalk

Sanderling Nature Center

Creeping Juniper Nature Trail Loop

Old Park Road

LAKE MICHIGAN

N

Legend

Park Office 🏠

Parking 🅿

Trail ▬

Intersecting Trail

Off-trail Route ✗✗✗✗

form a thick, dark line across the northern horizon stretching back to the west. Behind the barrier dune is a large, irregularly shaped valley dotted with juniper, a couple of white pine and a few brave birch. The place looks inviting, cozy, secretive.

Back on the cordwalk, the trail that had earlier split off reconnects. As you walk west, the dark line of trees that was visible from the bench gets closer. You'll walk past a "dune bottom" of about 2 acres that teems with vegetation. Apparently the low area is close enough to groundwater that trees and other plants can take root and survive in the sand. Aspen, pine, birch, mullein, milkweed, willow and dune grass all flourish together in this unlikely biotic community.

When you reach the edge of the tree line, the cordwalk splits again. The spur to the right leads 100 yards to a high spot on the dunes and a nice overlook of the beach below. Head straight and you'll enter a woods and reach the park's north parking lot.

If you head east from the parking area you'll find another cordwalk that takes you the 50 yards or so to the beach. Once there you have about 3.5 miles of inviting beach to explore: a half mile to the northern park boundary and three miles to the southern. To return to your car from here, retrace your steps on the cordwalk. It's .7 miles back to the parking lot. ▲

20

Saxon Harbor to
Graveyard Creek
Lake Superior Shoreline

*Trace the shoreline of a great inland sea
to one of Wisconsin's most remote places.*

Distance: Four miles round trip.

Time: Two to three hours in summer; four to five hours in winter.

Path: There is no path; you must find your own way along the sand beach pinned between Lake Superior and high, eroded cliffs. After big summertime rains, count on getting your feet wet at one or more of the creek mouths. In winter, snowshoes are essential, skis less utilitarian because of the ice and extremely uneven surface. Be extra careful finding firm ice when crossing the creeks.

Directions: From Highway 2 west of Hurley, head north on Highway 122 four miles to County A. Turn left on County A and drive one mile to the harbor and a parking area on the right.

Contact: None. For general information about the area, contact the Iron County Development Zone, 100 Cary Road, Hurley, WI 54534; (715) 561-2922. Steve Sorensen, co-owner of Northward Bookstore, also knows the area and is an articulate and willing conversationalist. Northward Bookstore is located at 410 W. Lake Shore Drive, Ashland, WI 54806; (715) 682-9772. For Bad River Reservation information, call (715) 682-7111.

Whether you trek its shores during high summer or deep winter, Lake Superior overwhelms everything else. The temperature can be 90 degrees in Mercer, 40 miles south, and, if there's a hint of north in the breeze, a thermometer at Saxon Harbor can read 65. A beautiful clear and sunny winter's day elsewhere, and snow might be piling up an inch an hour at Saxon Harbor.

This walk leads to one of the most remote places in Wisconsin—Graveyard Creek. The view from the creek's mouth takes in more than 30 miles of Lake Superior shoreline, from Little Girl's Point in

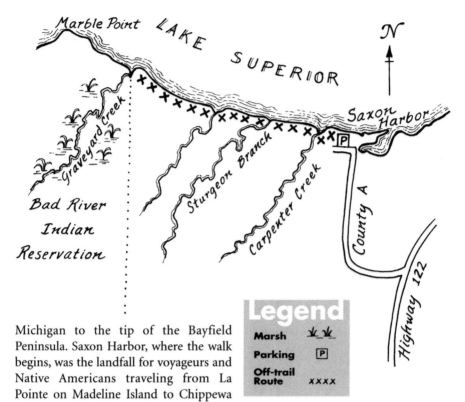

Michigan to the tip of the Bayfield Peninsula. Saxon Harbor, where the walk begins, was the landfall for voyageurs and Native Americans traveling from La Pointe on Madeline Island to Chippewa villages along the Flambeau and other interior rivers.

Head west from the parking lot on County A for a few hundred feet to a place where the beach is accessible down a gentle grade. In summer, the lake will draw you to her. You'll find walking in the loose sand wonderful, but sometimes difficult. In many places, the sand gives way to pebbles, zillions of pounded, rounded stones that have been sorted into similar sizes by wave action. Some piles are expansive, stretching 50 or more feet; some are small, one stride long. The stones in the water are the most striking. They glisten in more earth-tone colors than a rainbow ever imagined.

In winter, depending on the month and the season's fury, the lake's presence may be more subtle. Oronto Bay and the harbor may be full of pack ice, jumbled and insecure, but still. Only the slow rise and fall of the horizon, from swells in the super-chilled lake, betrays open water in the distance. You'll encounter icy, rounded balls in all sizes and in many degrees of opacity. Walking over them on snowshoes is difficult. Hope for snow cover.

Let your eyes follow the gentle curve of the shoreline as it moves west and you will see Marble Point, land's end from this vantage point. It's near the destination of this walk, Graveyard Creek, about three miles distant.

Check out the cliff face. The area is highly eroded, with trees and brush having tumbled lakeward. Close examination of the soil gives at least partial explanation. It's comprised of extremely fine reddish clay that turns to dust when exposed and rubbed. Snow that piles near the cliff in winter is tinged with this red color. The rouge tricks the eye, deepening shallow swales, causing you to place your snowshoe more cautiously then necessary.

About a half mile into the walk, you'll reach Carpenter Creek. A summer crossing is easy; often a big stride will suffice. In winter, exercise care so as not to break through the ice. Usually, the frozen jumble of pack ice is thickest and your best bet for crossing the creek's mouth.

It's less than another half mile to the next creek, Sturgeon Creek. Both it and the third stream—an unnamed little trickle a quarter of a mile farther—are less noticeable than Carpenter Creek and should offer no problems getting across.

As you approach the fourth creek, ominously named Graveyard, you may see a cabin on shore beyond the creek's west bank. Also note that the cliff face disappears here. It's interesting to observe that the headwaters of all these streams are all less then five miles from here, on the lake side of Highway 2.

Near Graveyard Creek and westward to Marble Point, the lake is more imminent. In summer, the waves are bigger, the roar louder. In winter, the lake is less distant here too, sometimes still splashing up through blowholes in the cold volcanolike cones it creates.

The mouth of Graveyard Creek marks the eastern boundary of the Bad River Indian Reservation. The Bad River Band of Chippewa have claimed riparian rights to the Lake Superior shoreline on their reservation. They do not want anyone other than tribal members on that shoreline.

So it's time to turn around. The return trip will retrace your route. But do not leave this beach before you fantasize for a moment about this place. Imagine Canadian wind crashing ashore, assaulting trees and cliffs and rocks. Think of the hundreds of ships that lie at the bottom of this great lake. Look at one of the trees above you and imagine it casting its seed below, onto the water. Seed that might root on Madeline Island or Grand Marais or Isle Royale. Feel how small you are. ▲

Riverside
Rambles

21

Along the Peshtigo
Goodman County Park

Amble on trail and off to experience a
roaring river, full of white water.

Distance: Two miles.

Time: One to two hours.

Path: Initially a worn footpath but not an easy one, muddy in spots, rocky and occasionally full of tree roots. Neither the trailhead nor the path are marked. The return walk, along the south bank of the river, does not follow a path—you must make your way through the woods.

Directions: From its junction with Highway 8 2.5 miles east of Goodman, take Parkway Road south approximately nine miles to Benson Lake Road. Turn right and proceed one mile to Goodman Park Road. Turn left; the park entrance is about .2 mile down the road on the right.

Contact: Marinette Chamber of Commerce, Box 512, 601 Marinette Ave., Marinette, WI 54143; (800) 236-6681.

The Peshtigo River is big and strong and full of white water. The stretch you'll walk along here is wonderfully typical. It's one of the few places where you can experience a long segment of this river without being on the water itself in a canoe or kayak, or having to walk a long way. Goodman Park is also a highlight of this walk. The substantial log buildings, built by the Civilian Conservation Corps between 1936 and 1938, are worth checking out.

Park in any of the several parking areas and begin your walk at the open shelter and signboard to the left of the park entrance road. The trail leads down to the river and two large log shelter houses. Strong Falls is straight ahead. While it lacks a big drop, the jumble of rocks splits the river and makes a nice display, especially at times of high water.

There's a bridge over the main river channel and another smaller one beyond. But instead of crossing them continue upstream along the bank. We will cross these bridges when we come to them, at the end of our walk.

The path is well-worn along the riverbank. It may be wet in places. It will take you past several small, room-sized islands, each full of small trees. One tree, a yellow birch, straddles two islands, roots firmly planted in both, doing the splits over the river below.

Above the islands, the river is quiet for a while, until it bends. As you begin to circle the outside edge of the bend, you'll hear the rapids upstream, before you see them. From a distance, they look frothy and playful. As you round the bend and approach the first of three sets of rapids, they become more impressive. If you were in a canoe, the big standing waves could dump you.

As a landlubber, your challenge is to keep your feet dry. There are several spots along the trail that could be wet. Indeed, at high water in the spring, the trail may be under water. If so, just head to the right, up the moderate slope, into the pine and spruce plantations. Keep the river in view (or within earshot), and you'll have no trouble finding your way.

You'll pass an island in the river. If you can get close enough to the bank to look at the island, notice the five different channels that present themselves to bewildered paddlers. Three giant boulders funnel the stream left (and block a paddler's view to the right). The three middle channels appear blocked by fallen trees. The right channel looks good, but hiding behind those giant boulders is a fallen tree and another big rock, both in position to capture a canoe or kayak. The channel next to where you've been walking looks the best, although there's a submerged rock and small eddy at its entrance. Be glad you're walking!

Swede John Road and a bridge over the river are just up the trail. Climb the steep, grassy hillside onto the road and cross the river. Look upstream toward more serious rapids and a falls that you can't see but to which you'll walk next.

Across the bridge and about 20 yards down the road, there's a well-worn path that cuts into the woods on the right. Follow this. It enters the woods on the side of the slope leading up from the river, but soon dips down and follows the river along its bank. You'll pass a long, narrow island separated from you by an almost jumpable trickle of water. At the upstream end of this island there's a surprise: a falls bigger and more impressive than Strong Falls. As you walk along the bank, look for a rock that juts out into the river. This rock and attendant hunk of earth is the perfect place to view the falls. Although only about 6 feet high, boulders conspire to pinch the river to less than half its width at the falls, assuring that plenty of water crashes through a small space. Up close, the falls is noisy and will spray you if the wind is right.

One more side trip. Although this is not an area of big impressive trees because of the way the county manages its forest, about 70 yards farther upstream from the falls and one-third of the way up the hillside from the river, there's a big-toothed aspen that's about 3 feet in diameter. It stands out all the more because of the puny ones around it, evidence that this tree is a surviver of multiple logging operations. Go over and give the tree a hug. It's one lucky aspen!

Head back to Swede John Road. You can retrace your footsteps near the river, or climb up-slope and try to follow the crest. Logging has made footing uneasy on the top of the slope, but it is walkable. When you get to the road, cross it and head into the woods directly across from where you earlier dove into the woods to see the falls. There is no path. The key is to keep the river in view or within earshot. It will bend away from the slope you're on, a wet floodplain filling the area below you. Stay on the side of the slope. It's covered with small ash, maple and yellow birch. Shade tolerant balsam fir have seeded in underneath. Walking is easy. Much of this north-facing slope also is covered with club moss and princess pine, two mosses often found together but rarely in such abundance. It's a soft, exotic carpet.

It's important that you keep the river in view because, when the river makes its bend back toward the slope you're on, you need to look for the bridges that you saw at the beginning of the walk or any other sign of the park. The buildings are easy to pick out if you stay toward the bottom of the slope. When you see the bridge or the buildings, head to them. After crossing the bridges, you'll be back where you started. Now when your friends brag about paddling the mighty Peshtigo, you can say you've walked it! ▲

Legend

Waterfall	⅏
Marsh	⩊
Bridge	⇒⩸
Parking	P
Off-trail Route	xxxx

22

Eau Claire Dells Segment of the Ice Age National Scenic Trail

Enjoy fine views of a fast river as it splashes through a deep gorge.

Distance: Five miles round trip.

Time: Three hours round trip.

Path: Well traveled and hilly, with rocks and roots that reach up and trip you. Trail marking is outstanding: yellow metal arrows and nameplates, with supplemental yellow blazes on trees. Up-to-date maps are posted at junctions. Other signs describe geological and natural history.

Directions: From the junction of Highway 29 and County Q 10 miles east of Wausau, take County Q north six miles to County Z. Turn right and go three miles to County Y. Turn left and go 1.5 miles north to the park entrance, which is on the left.

Contact: Ice Age Park and Trail Foundation
P.O. Box 423, Pewaukee, WI 53072; (414) 691-2776.

The Dells of the Eau Claire is a state natural area, so designated because of its exemplary flora, which is a mixed-hardwood/conifer community. The area also contains interesting geology. Here the river runs a deep gorge that was cut through 1.5 billion-year-old mylonite rock by millennia of rushing waters.

Enter the Woods Trail from the picnic area, .3 miles from the park entrance. The canopy is of wonderful northern hardwoods: sugar maple, red oak, white ash and basswood, many with trunks so big you can't touch your fingers around the other side when you hug them. Orange columbine flowers punctuate the green forest floor, which is carpeted in places by the big, dark-green (almost blue) leaves of wild ginger.

Soon the hardwoods give way to hemlock, those large evergreens with the small needles and cones. The trail becomes dark and damp as almost nothing grows under hemlocks. Then the canopy changes again, aspen providing the shade between a couple of small clearings. You'll come to a trail post and sign. From here, be sure to follow the yellow Ice Age Trail markers. (See the Introduction for more on the IAT.)

A hundred feet beyond the sign, the path drops down a series of rock ledges, off what is called High Bluff. You can hear the river as you approach the bridge that crosses the Eau Claire. High Bridge is an old bridge, built with lots of sweat, wood on pillars of native rock stacked like blocks and rising out of the streambed.

"Nature is a mutable cloud, always and never the same." Rivers are an immutable part of nature, so it's likely Emerson would agree, rivers are all the same, yet different. From High Bridge, boulders and bedrock extrusions, polished by cascades of water, dot the river's east-west channel. The slate-gray rock, almost black when wet, is lightened by touches of blue and green; the latter is moss and, occasionally, lichen that somehow manages to eke out an existence on the rock. The river's splashing is matched by its glistening dance, sunlight reflected off chaotic surfaces.

About 150 feet past High Bridge, the Ice Age Trail veers right from the county park trails. Big white pine, 3 feet or more in diameter, shelter the riverside for the next 500 feet. Some equally large hemlock also contribute their shade.

After a quarter mile, the trail goes by a 3-foot-high river ledge where water gushes noisily. The river parts here, most of it flowing around the other side of an island that looms ahead. An eddy formed by the rock ledge and a little curve in the river creates a small, dark pool, a place for smallmouth bass. Below a fern-covered rock outcrop, just on the edge of the river, you'll notice an unusual tree. It's small, 15 feet tall, and multistemmed with a leaf that resembles a maple. Most outstanding is its flower, which is a spikelike affair that sticks straight up in the air from the branch tips. This is a mountain maple (*Acer spicatum*).

In another quarter mile, the canopy opens for the first time, letting unfiltered sunlight strike the ground. Then the canopy closes again. A logging road snakes off to the left, climbing the incline away from the river. On the right side of the trail, a gnarled old white pine scratches its way skyward from a clump of rock. Next to the tree is a terraced arrangement of rock ledges that is more comfortable than many chairs. Have a seat. Someone's cut dead lower branches from the pine, making this spot even more inviting. The river courses 30 feet below, fast and noisy. Enjoy the small yellow birch stand that clings precipitously to the thin soil. Sit quietly and you may see the mink that hunts here. Look for its scat, full of shells, along the rock ledge.

Look for human handiwork a few hundred yards farther down the trail. Someone has paved a 15-foot-long walkway to the river with native stone. It's a pleasant invitation and entrance to big slabs of flat bedrock along which the river tumbles.

A short distance past the walkway, the trail traverses its first lowland area. Black ash and alder are everywhere, along with some sedges and other marsh grasses. A bridge carries you across the wettest spot.

Soon you'll cross an extensive open area with 30-foot-tall big tooth aspen, balsam fir and red maple. On a sunny day the temperature rises several degrees in this opening compared to the mature woods.

The canopy closes again as you enter a different woodland type, this one occupied by lots of bur oak. After the trail turns left, away from the river, other trails begin to intersect. The grass shows signs of tire tracks. Then the trail is mowed! When you hear traffic, you are almost to County Z. When you reach the road, reverse direction and retrace your steps to your car. ▲

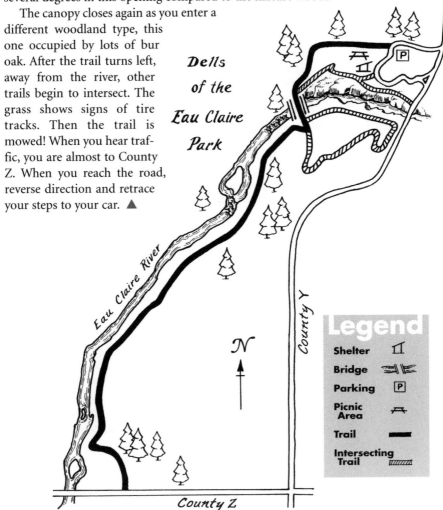

Dells of the Eau Claire Park

Eau Claire River

N

County Y

County Z

Legend

Shelter	🛖
Bridge	▱◺
Parking	P
Picnic Area	🪑
Trail	▬
Intersecting Trail	▨

23

Lagoo Creek Route
Governor Knowles State Forest

*Visit the historic St. Croix, site
of huge 19th-century log drives.*

Distance: Three miles round trip.

Time: One to one and a half hours.

Path: The path down the escarpment is loose sand, between wooden steps. It's a difficult descent. On the river floodplain, the path is a worn, sandy trail. It is marked with walker signs, arrows and blue blazes.

Directions: From the intersection of Highway 87 and Evergreen Avenue approximately 13 miles south of Grantsburg, take Evergreen Avenue 12 miles west to the parking area.

Contact: Governor Knowles State Forest
P.O. Box 367, Grantsburg, WI 54840; (715) 463-2898.

This walk has an inauspicious beginning. The area around the parking lot and along the first quarter mile or so of the trail was logged in 1995. Yet on a late summer morning the bluebirds trill and dart between stump sprouts and the few larger pine left standing, and make the place seem friendly and less barren. Once you enter the uncut woods, you become aware of the St. Croix flowing on your left, down the hill past lots of trees. A large semicircular gully appears on the left, nearly touching the trail. You're standing on top of a spring. Water gurgles out below you, into a small stream that tumbles toward the bigger river.

The river bottom floodplain soon comes into view. The trail down onto the floodplain is difficult because it's steep and the sand between the wood steps is loose. Near the bottom of your descent, you'll hear water rushing down a small stream that meets the trail. As you cross the makeshift wooden bridge over this creek, another waterway is visible below you. From your vantage point above it, you can see its dark tan, sand-filled, rippled bottom, and its route through the riverine forest, almost to where it empties into the St. Croix.

Now that you're off the escarpment, you'll begin crossing intermittent creeks. Some of these are less than a couple of hundred feet long, beginning as springs cascading out of the escarpment wall. The first ones you'll cross by stepping on strategically placed rocks. Another is spanned by a footbridge. Note the longer, deeper valley upstream. The St. Croix River is closer now, and at about the same level as the trail. There's another bridge, then a third, and suddenly the trail has you up on the riverbank. This is your first chance to get a good view of the St. Croix. Step off the path and walk the 30 feet or so to the river. Here the St. Croix is broad, flat and swift. In the last century, the river was a major transportation route for the lumber companies. In the spring of 1865, it carried more than two hundred million feet of logs to the sawmills. During spring log drives, pine tree trunks would be so thick that they would clog the river. A person could literally walk across to the other bank.

The bank you're walking on is interesting. It's about 3 feet high and very uniform. It looks unnatural, as if the river was dredged. But there are 18-inch-diameter, multistemmed silver maple growing on it, stump-sprouted progeny of much larger trees that stood here for more than a hundred years. Why is the bank so defined, so humped up? One theory says that ice pushed up the soil over the course of hundreds of years. Another theory

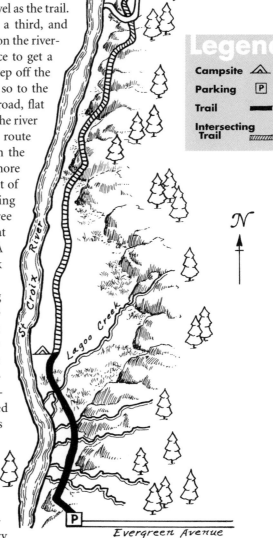

75

says the bank was deformed by logs battering against it during log drives. Whatever the reason, the slope and high grasses make walking along the river difficult.

Walk away from the river to regain the trail, and note that a wet ravine is now on your right, between you and the escarpment. The area you're walking through would be submerged during periods of high water. When you get to a spot·where there are many white pine, walk off the trail back over to the St. Croix. Several big old white pine sit atop that high bank. These trees are about a hundred years old.

An intermittent game trail goes upriver and makes a convenient walking path for a few hundred feet through the pines. Eventually, you'll want to once again put the river to your back and walk away from it to return to the main walking trail.

Continue on down the trail, paying attention to the blue blazes on the trees. The trail will move away from the St. Croix briefly to cross Lagoo Creek via a wooden bridge. (If you miss the blazes, you'll arrive at Lagoo nearer the St. Croix. There's an unofficial campsite where the creek joins the river, but no bridge.)

After the trail crosses the bridge, it enters a broad, mostly open area of wet floodplain. The vegetation is very different here, with grasses and sedges dominating. The trail traces a course between this wet floodplain area and the base of the now 15-foot-high riverbank. Climb the bank for another view of the river and a visit to a developed canoe campsite, complete with fire ring and pit toilets.

From this point, the trail continues for seven miles to a parking lot at County O and keeps going for seven more miles beyond that. This walk turns around here; retrace your steps to the Evergreen Avenue parking lot. ▲

24

Parfrey's Glen Trail
Parfrey's Glen State Natural Area

Stroll into a tranquil glen
enhanced by a charming creek.

Distance: About one mile round trip.

Time: One hour.

Path: Other than signs at the beginning of the trail and a few informational signs, there is no marking, but the path is easy to follow. It has a slight grade with some stone steps.

Directions: From the intersection of Highway 113 and County DL (Parfrey's Glen Road) about eight miles southeast of Baraboo, take County DL east approximately two miles to the parking area, which is on the left.

Contact: Devil's Lake State Park
S5975 Park Road, Baraboo, WI 53913; (608) 356-8301.

The sheer rock walls that enclose Parfrey's Glen are striking, but it's the gurgle of the brook bouncing off those walls that makes a sensual impression.

The first quarter of the walk is on a broad gravel roadbed through a partially wooded field. On a late August day, textures catch the eye. Fine spikes of goldenrod ripen seed amid slightly courser staghornless sumac. Above stands a wall of white pine fronds, solid but soft looking, with the billowy leaves of poplar topping the tapestry. You can hear the creek here also, as you cross over the culverted cascade, more pleasing to the ear than the eye.

As the road grade steepens a bit, the woods thicken around you. Woodland sunflowers, asters and more goldenrod persist in open areas along the road. Some large white cedar line the creek on the left, and make the place seem more northern.

Finally the road narrows to a rustic path of fine stone, lined on each side by logs. You'll walk over the first of several wooden bridges. If you fix your gaze on the rushing water long enough, it will seem like the water is standing still while the beachball-sized rocks are rolling down the stream. An impressive stand of jewelweed glows orange at the base of the glen wall, which is just beginning to define itself.

Another bridge spans the creek bed. On the left side as you leave the bridge, there's a blue beech tree *(Carpinus caroliniana)* with a diameter of about 6 inches—unusually large for this species. There are many smaller such trees in the area. The blue beech is also known as muscle wood because of its smooth, musclelike gray bark.

Water seeps down an embankment just ahead of a sign that honors Norman Carter Fassett, who chaired the state Natural Area Committee from 1945 to 1950, and who selected Parfrey's Glen as the state's first natural area. The glen is unusual in that it contains plant species rarely found this far south.

When you see some sandstone outcrops on the left, you're nearing steps that will take you into another world. The steps have been hewn from native stone and fit the site perfectly. They present a modest climb, perhaps 20 feet, but suddenly you're in a canyon with sheer rock walls 40 feet high. The closest wall, on your left, has odd strata. Layered between homogenous sandstone are 6- to 12-inch layers of small pebbles and stones. The layers are called conglomerate sandstone and were formed in the Cambrian era. At that time, the Baraboo Hills were islands in a sea. The rounded rocks in the conglomerate—quartzite—were eroded from the islands and rolled about in the waves. As the sea level rose, some were deposited on the shores and covered by sand and other marine sediments, which also completely buried the islands. Today, erosion again (from Parfrey's Glen Creek), has uncovered these "islands" and the mix of pebbles and boulders.

In the canyon, you'll walk on a succession of bridges and piers over and along the creek. White pine hang precipitously to the cliff edge 30 feet above you. Stop occasionally and gaze down into pools in the

Parfrey's Glen

Legend

Parking   P

Trail   ▬

Intersecting Trail   ▨

N ↑

Creek

P

Parfrey's Glen Road

creek for native brook trout. Make sure you wait, looking carefully near the edges of submerged rocks, in quiet places near fast current. There are a lot of trout here; if you don't see one, you probably haven't looked long enough.

As you move farther up the glen, it narrows to a width of 15, maybe 20 feet, with sheer rock walls. Sometimes turkeys flap across the gap above you as they traverse the surrounding hillsides looking for food and for each other.

When you come to a jumble of big rocks that have fallen from the side of the glen into the creek, you're almost to the end of the trail. It's marked with an unambiguous "Trail Ends" sign and a modest rock wall. You can hear and see a 5-foot falls at the head of the glen. Beyond the falls there is no more canyon visible, just upland. You have reached the top of the glen. One more sight awaits you though. Look up at the rock ledge just overhead of the spot where the trail widens to make its little rock ledge. Reaching out over the trail is a mountain maple. In the spring, these trees have 4-inch spikes of greenish-yellow flowers that stand erect from the branches. The mountain maple is a very unusual tree to find this far south, and there are several of these trees above you here.

To return to the parking lot, turn around and retrace your steps along the trail. ▲

25

Perry Creek Trail
Perry Creek Recreation Area
Black River Falls State Forest

A quick walk along a pleasant little river.

Distance: Three-quarters of a mile round trip.

Time: Forty-five minutes.

Path: A worn footpath, mostly on a carpet of leaves, needles and bark. The terrain is flat, but there are obstacles such as fallen trees.

Directions: From the intersection of Highway 54 and Highway 27 east of Black River Falls, take Highway 27 south 2.5 miles to Perry Creek Road. Turn right on Perry Creek Road and drive about a mile to its end at a boat launch and picnic area parking lot.

Contact: Wisconsin Department of Natural Resources 910 Highway 54E, Black River Falls, WI 54615; (715) 284-1400.

This short walk begins from the parking lot next to the Black River boat landing at the end of Perry Creek Road. Head east, across the picnic area, and you'll see Perry Creek. The trail begins at the Religious Footbridge, so christened because it takes faith to cross this rickety suspension bridge. At this point, Perry Creek is making its way hurriedly down the last hundred feet until it loses itself in the Black River.

The falls are about 50 yards down the trail. You can hear them as soon as you cross the bridge. They span 15 feet across the little creek and make a 4-foot drop. The cave 20 feet downstream on the opposite bank is fascinating. Here, the water has swirled a circular depression deep into the rock, undercutting the bank.

The trail leads farther upstream, and the creek gorge deepens. By the time you reach a wooden bridge, you have to tilt your head to see the top of the rock layer cake that hems in the creek.

Past the bridge, the trail cuts up the hillside, and a series of steps takes you to an upland where you walk about 50 feet above the level of the creek. Then the trail heads down to the creek again and is

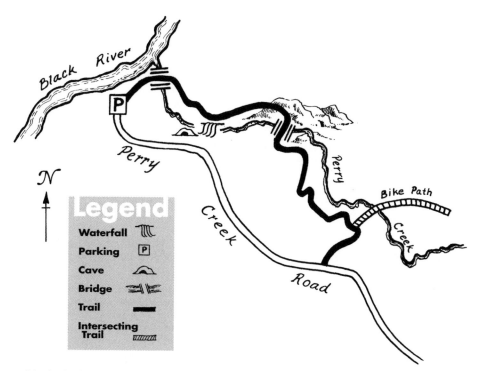

blocked where a spring flood piled debris 12 feet high across the creek bed. White pine, 2 to 3 feet in diameter, lie crossed, jammed against one another and other flotsam. A 9-inch iron I-beam juts out of the jumble. It's part of a bridge that used to cross the creek just 50 yards upstream. If the big trees and jumble of debris don't attest to the water's fury, the bend in the I-beam does.

You can pick your way through the debris and continue on the path another 50 yards to its intersection with Perry Creek Road. To get back to the parking lot, turn around and retrace your route. ▲

26

Tower Hill Hiking Trail
Tower Hill State Park

Step back in time on a walk to a historic shot tower,
enhanced by lovely views of the Wisconisn River.

Distance: One mile.

Time: One hour.

Path: Difficult terrain, with a steep hill and old, frost-heaved stonework. Old maps are located at key intersections but are faded and disfigured so don't rely on them.

Directions: From the intersection of Highway 23 and County C south of Spring Green, go east on County C one mile to the park entrance, which is on the left. Follow the park road to the campground. The trailhead is between campsites 12 and 13. A state park sticker is required.

Contact: Tower Hill State Park
Route 3, Spring Green, WI 53588; (608) 588-2116.

The highlights of this walk are a lovely view of the Wisconsin River Valley and a hike down to Mill Creek along a sandstone cliff face. The hand-dug tunnels through the cliff are also amazing, and you get to walk into one of them. A restored tower that was used in the mid-1800s to make lead shot is fascinating.

Start your walk on the blacktop path between campsites 12 and 13. When you reach the flagstone steps, begin looking to the left. Even when the leaves are on the trees you can catch some nice views of the Wisconsin River Valley, Spring Green and Mill Creek below. A chain-link fence protects you from falling off the cliff face and into the creek.

You'll come to some steps that go right, farther up the hill. These lead to the shot tower and you'll come back to them later. For now, head down the trail and follow the steps down to where the chain-link becomes wood railing and the trail switches back down the hillside. At this switchback, you may notice a glossy, green vinelike plant at your feet. This is a non-native periwinkle, out of place but pretty.

Continue down the hill on the frost-heaved steps until you reach the creek bed and the entrance to the shot tower tunnel. You'll pass some large white pine on your way and walk alongside layered sandstone. The tunnel, dug by hand, reaches about 25 yards deep into the hillside. It's just over 6 feet tall, wide, circular and dark! Most days there's a breeze blowing out of the tunnel. Walk inside carefully because you can't see much until your eyes adjust to the darkness. At the back of the tunnel is a steel grate, beyond which is the vertical shaft from the shot tower. You'll be able to read about it from up top at the display in the restored tower.

There's also a bridge across Mill Creek here. The trail ends on the other side of the bridge because the area beyond is in the creek's floodplain and often too wet for good walking. Walk out onto the bridge anyway because it affords you a neat view of the bare rock face jutting out over the creek. Sixty feet above, a big white pine sticks out over the creek, holding on with roots that will eventually fracture the rock they cling to, causing all to tumble into the creek.

Legend

Park Office	⌂
Parking	Ⓟ
Campsite	△
Bridge	⟊⟊
Trail	▬
Intersecting Trail	⬚

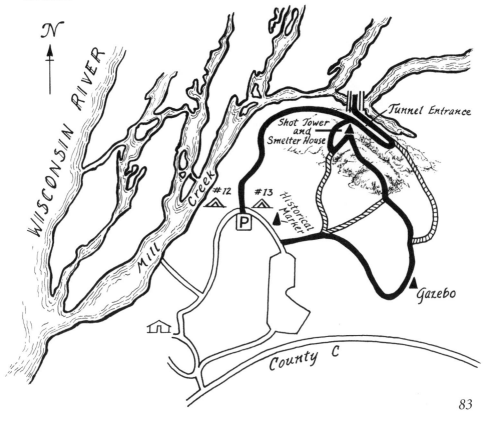

N

WISCONSIN RIVER

Mill Creek

Tunnel Entrance

Shot Tower and Smelter House

#12

#13

Historical Marker

P

Gazebo

County C

Take the same route up that you just came down on, back to the stairs that lead to the tower. Bear left onto them. Your first stop is at the bottom of the tower, where the stone shaft begins. Walk inside and look down the 120-foot-deep hole. It took two men 187 days to complete the shaft. Think about digging such a shaft. It makes the walk up these stairs seem easy.

Follow the steps and dirt path farther up, around the tower to the asphalt path above. This is the Old Ox Nature Trail, and if you go left when you reach it, you'll climb another 50 feet or so to the tower, built in 1831. Inside is a display and explanation of how and why the tower was built. Local lead mines provided the raw material for manufacturing lead shot. Melted lead was dropped from the top of the shot tower; the droplets cooled and became round as they fell. After drying, polishing and sorting, the lead was barged down Mill Creek to the Wisconsin River, the Mississippi and, its final destination, St. Louis.

Outside, follow the trail around the tower to the fence that overlooks the river valley. Below you lies a section of the Lower Wisconsin State Riverway. This 92-mile-long segment, from the dam at Prairie du Sac to the river's confluence with the Mississippi at Prairie du Chien, is the longest free-flowing section of river anywhere in the Midwest. From your perch you can see the village of Spring Green across the river, and the five green spans of the Highway 14 bridge. You can also notice how wide the river valley is by noting the elevated Highway 14 roadway before it gets to the bridge. It is almost a mile in length.

After you've visited the displays inside the tower, continue your walk down the path toward the gazebo. The path becomes narrow and a bit brushy as it snakes down the hillside. Below the gazebo you'll walk through a grove of black locust trees, then some large oak until you reach the park road. Campsites 12 and 13 are just a hundred yards to your right. ▲

The
Glacier's
Path

11·15·97.
Snow, Cold·

27

Circle Loop Trail
Chippewa Moraine Ice Age
National Scientific Reserve

Eskers, seepage lakes and an unusual
ice-walled lake plain highlight a walk
dotted with spring wildflowers.

Distance: 4.5 miles.

Time: Two to three hours.

Path: Well-worn, moss-covered earth (slippery when moist) over hilly terrain. Marking is excellent, with yellow diamond signs or yellow blazes on trees. An excellent map is available at the trailhead.

Directions: From County M and Highway 53 in New Auburn, take County M east 5 3/4 miles. Enter at the Interpretive Center entrance, which is on the left.

Contact: Chippewa Moraine Interpretive Center
13394 County M, New Auburn, WI 54757; (715) 967-2800.

Lakes, lakes and more lakes! More than 70 lakes dot the Chippewa Moraine reserve: 12 percent of all the lakes in Chippewa County. The parking lot at the Interpretive Center is on the bottom of a lake, albeit on the top of one of the highest hills in the reserve. Fifteen thousand years ago, glacial meltwater, walled in by debris-covered ice, formed a tublike lake. When the ice wall melted, the lake drained, leaving behind a high plain, which geologists call an "ice-walled lake plain." Today, that broad plateau offers great views to the south and west.

Before starting your walk, visit the Interpretive Center. It has wonderful exhibits that more fully explain the geology of the area, as well as the flora and fauna.

Our walk begins just to the north of the center. We're going to walk the 4.5-mile Circle Loop in a counterclockwise direction. The first quarter mile or so is also a nature trail. You'll pass a sign that exhorts you to "slow down" and relax. Not a bad idea. The trail's downhill

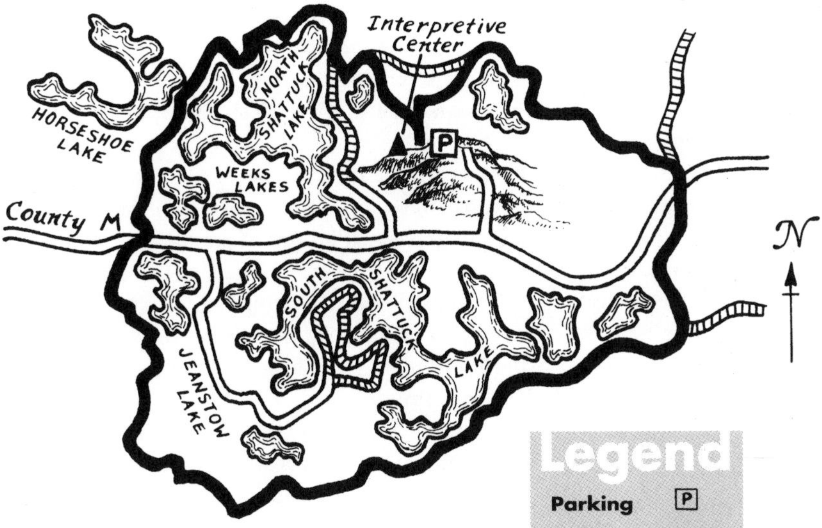

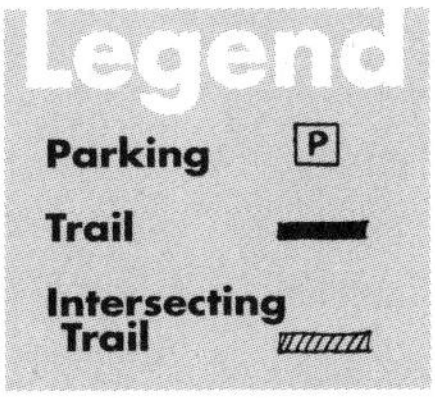

pitch helps you appreciate the height of the ice-walled plain.

The woods is big, with lots of large oaks. The understory is raspberry, hazelnut, alder, other northern shrubs and an assortment of wildflowers, including trillium, columbine and violet. Ten minutes or so into your walk you'll encounter an area of blown-over trees, mostly aspen, but oak also. A big wind in June 1995 pushed them down.

You'll cross a wood bridge that spans an odd gully between two lakes. Take a minute and look at the gully from the bridge. Very straight, with uniform ridges on both edges, it wasn't gouged out by a glacier. It was dug by lumberjacks. Because the terrain here is so hilly, loggers sometimes made channels between two lakes to create a level passage. In winter, oxen pulled sleds full of big pine logs through these "sledways" to landing areas. In spring, the logs were floated down-river to the sawmills.

Just past the bridge, there's a thick stand of mapleleaf viburnum, a 3- to 5-foot shrub that, while common throughout the state, is almost unknown. That's because it looks like a maple tree seedling. It's most conspicuous in fall, when it turns a wonderful shade of mauve.

The trail winds by several lakes, including North Shattuck, Horseshoe and Weeks lakes. These were all created by glacial action. They are seepage lakes, which means that, rather than being drained by rivers, their water flows in and out through the groundwater system. Levels have fluctuated by a couple of feet over the last 20 years.

Most of these lakes are shallow, subject to winter kill and essentially fishless. But what's bad for fish is good for reptiles like frogs and sala- manders, which can lay eggs without worrying about themselves and their little hatchlings becoming fish food. Keep an ear open for frog songs here.

After you cross County M, the trail winds around the west end of Jeanstow Lake and heads south, up onto a 15-foot-high esker. The esker formed as sand and gravel settled out of a meltwater river that tunneled under the glacier. The area was logged in the early 1990s, before it was sold to the state. Some of the big red oak stumps reveal more than 170 rings. In June, wild geranium carpet the area, purple- blue flowers drinking in sunlight. Hillsides open to more light are covered with stands of interrupted fern.

Once back into unlogged woods, you'll come upon more lakes. You'll stroll for more than a quarter of a mile along the southeast shore of South Shattuck Lake. If the mosquitoes and/or deer flies are thick, you may jog or run and not stroll.

At the next junction, .2 mile past South Shattuck Lake, the Ice Age Trail heads off to the east toward Plummer Lake. You will turn left, continuing the Circle Loop.

An uphill climb through a red pine plantation marks the approach to County M. This road crossing also is well-marked. The trail passes a couple of more lakes and crosses two bridges before it begins the climb up the hill to the Interpretive Center. Pause for a moment, gaze up the hill through big oaks, and think about standing under 120 feet of ice. ▲

28

Holy Hill Segment
of the Ice Age
National Scenic Trail

*See the soaring spires of Holy Hill
as you clamber up kames and moraines.*

Distance: Three miles.

Time: Two to four hours.

Path: A well-worn trail with some steep, but not precipitous, climbs over heavily wooded glacial topography. Wet, boggy places appear in the spring and after rainfall. There is poison ivy in the area, too, so don't go prancing off into the woods without caution and long pants. The trail is well marked with Ice Age Trail yellow blazes and posts painted yellow on top. Two spur trails are blazed in blue.

Directions: From the Highway 41/45 and Highway 167 interchange, go west approximately 8.5 miles to Stations Way Road, then left on Stations Way .2 mile to the parking area at the picnic grounds. If you reach the Holy Hill entrance sign at Carmel Road, you have gone too far on Highway 167.

Contact: Ice Age Park and Trail Foundation
P.O. Box 423, Pewaukee, WI 53072; (414) 691-2776.

Anyone who has seen the spires of Holy Hill from one of the many roads leading to it will appreciate the incredible views along this trail. The spires rise from the National Shrine of Mary, Help of Christians, which is administered by Carmelite friars. The hill upon which the church stands is so named because a French hermit experienced a miraculous cure here in the mid-1800s. Holy Hill is also one of the largest, if not the largest, kame in Wisconsin. (A kame is a conical mound that forms at the bottom of a hole in a glacier.) The view from one of the church spires is breathtaking—literally so on a windy day.

The best place to start this walk is from the picnic area just off Stations Way Road. The Ice Age Trail enters the woods from the northeast corner. (See the Introduction for more on the Ice Age Trail.)

After crossing a short footbridge over some wet spots, you'll walk through an old clearing. Look for the abandoned farmstead on the right. Soon you'll be in the midst of an old apple orchard, overtopped by 25- to 30-year-old basswood, elm and other trees.

A second bridge takes you past a wet, open glade on the right side of the trail. This is a place for wildflowers. In early spring, marsh marigolds hold forth in yellow splendor.

A small lake lies to the left of the third and last bridge. From here you'll climb some steps, past a couple of bur and white oaks, to a bench. When leafless, the trees allow a view of a kame to the east.

After more climbing, a spur trail leads off to the right. This couple-hundred-yard trail makes a serious climb up a kame to a viewpoint that looks west toward the church. If the leaves are on the trees, the view is obscured.

The main trail continues southwest, also gains altitude, and arrives at a bench with a magnificent view of the hill and church. The three spires soar skyward, but the church itself is not much higher than you are. This is one of only two vantage points (Lapham Peak, 20 miles south, is the other) from which you are looking across at the church, not up at it!

Pause to imagine how thick the glacier was that created this topography. The middle church tower is 192 feet tall. Geologists maintain that the glacier was about a thousand feet thick. Try visualizing four more towers stacked on top of the one there and you'll sense the enormity of the ice cube that ate Wisconsin 10,000 years ago.

Off again, you'll plunge down the kame that provided such a great view, in search of the next glimpse of the church. You'll cross a snowmobile trail and traverse a small opening full of sumac and small elm. You'll step across a nifty manmade rock culvert that channels runoff from the hillside harmlessly past the trail. Then it's back to the woods and up another ridge. Near the top, blue blazes take you left, farther up the ridge to another bench and view.

Back on the main trail, you'll traverse 23 wide steps up to the near-summit of a long east-west running ridge (possibly a moraine—cast-off glacial debris) to your final view of the church. The trail runs due west along the base of this ridge for the next quarter mile or so. (Look for gigantic grapevines that snake their way across the ground and up the trees.) You'll make a left turn and walk up and over a saddle in the ridge. The trail snakes down the other side of the ridge through a pine woods, then takes you past large sugar maple trees, through a plantation of white pine and finally out onto Donegal Road. Turkeys are frequent visitors to this section of trail so be sure to look for them.

You can turn around and retrace your steps to the parking area (about 1.5 miles) or you can make a loop by walking west on Donegal Road less than a quarter of a mile to Carmel Road. Turn right on Carmel Road. It's about half a mile to the entrance of the Holy Hill complex. If you're not tired of climbing, walk .2 mile up the entrance road to see the church. Once there, if you're still not tired of climbing, visit the church's tower and climb its 178 stairs to the exposed viewing platform. (Tip: If it's cold and windy, wear a jacket.) If visibility permits, you'll drink in views—looking southeast to southwest—of the downtown Milwaukee skyline, the hills of the Southern Kettle Moraine State Forest, Lapham Peak and the Nagawicka lakes area. To the north, a slightly misshapen cone is Powder Hill, a kame in Pike Lake State Park.

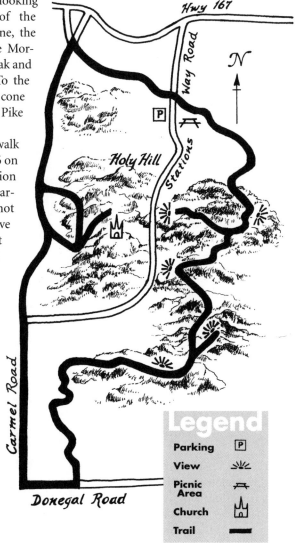

One caution about the walk up the tower. Rule Number 6 on the scenic tower information sheet says: "The stairs are narrow and steep. Please do not climb the stairs if you have breathing problems, heart problems, a fear of enclosed places or a fear of heights." Enough said!

To continue your loop back to the picnic parking area, head north on Carmel Road (a right turn out of the Holy Hill entrance road). In a bit more than a quarter mile and just before a guardrail begins, take a right turn onto the Ice Age Trail. The trail skirts a long, thin cattail marsh on the left before exiting in 300 yards into the picnic area and this walk's starting point. ▲

Legend

Parking	P
View	☀
Picnic Area	🛆
Church	⛪
Trail	▬

29

Lodi Segment
of the Ice Age
National Scenic Trail

Walk along a glacier-scraped ridge
to sweeping views of hills and valleys.

Distance: 4.8 miles.

Time: Three hours round trip.

Path: Well-maintained and marked with yellow blazes. The terrain is hilly but not steep. Beware of poison ivy; in some places it is so thick that it's difficult to walk without touching it with your shoes.

Directions: From Highway 60, just south of Lodi, take Riddle Road south. The trailhead is .5 mile down. However, you will need to drive about a half mile farther to a parking lot and then walk back up the road to the trailhead.

Contact: Ice Age Park and Trail Foundation
P.O. Box 423, Pewaukee, WI 53072; (414) 691-2776.

This walk on the Ice Age Trail provides nice overlooks of the topography: hills, valleys and bluffs. (See the Introduction for more on the IAT.) While there are some wonderful woods, the meadows stand out as inviting, open places, full of lushness.

Negotiating the narrow Z-shaped fence entrance to the trail is the most difficult part of this hike. Constructed to prevent entry by vehicles, the short but effective maze is a little tricky, even for walkers.

After a brief stint through a grassy field, the trail enters a thick woods and you'll begin a climb up to a ridgetop. This ridge, and others that you will walk along, were all scraped by the glacier. Composed of hard limestone bedrock, the hills took a beating from the ice but didn't succumb entirely. As it crept into this area, the glacier carried with it lots of ground sandstone and other rock (which it had picked up farther north), mixed this with locally gathered material, and left it all behind here after it melted. This created a rich medium for the growth of diverse native plants. In early June, delicate, light-blue wild geranium carpet the forest. Unfortunately, non-natives flourish too, and much of the understory is composed in places entirely of buckthorn, a plant used for ornamental purposes that's gotten out of hand.

When you pass under the powerline, you've come about a half mile and are near the first meadow. Wade through the deep grass and wildflower sea and gradually climb up to a point where there's a view back to the north and northwest. Between you and the horizon, you'll see a large mound called Gibralter Rock. Beyond that are the undulations of the Baraboo Hills. You'll also note a house and other buildings off to the left of the trail just beyond the overlook. The trail comes close to private property here.

For the next .3 miles or so, the trail sits atop a broad plateau. You may see many small, charred trees with copious root sprouts. Ice Age Trail workers have set fires here in an effort to establish an oak savannah. Plants that grow in a savannah, including the fire-resistant bur oak, require full sunlight.

When you arrive at Dave's Overlook check out

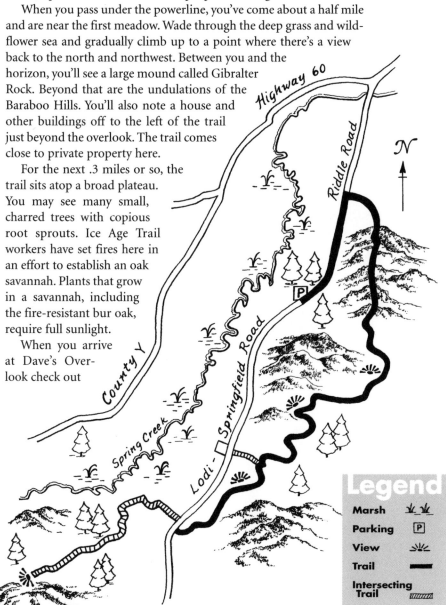

the westerly view. In the distance, you'll see the "Devil's Nose"—the east end of the south bluff at Devil's Lake State Park. Hiking away from Dave's Overlook, you'll pass through a "sumac tunnel," where this small, profusely suckering tree has established a dense thicket. It's a spectacular tunnel when wrapped in the orange and red leaves of fall. The tunnel leads you to a woods and a descent. As you pop out of the woods, look over the valley in front of you and you can see the trail as it winds across the next hillside. The intervening valley is full of interesting plants. In one hundred-yard stretch you can see St. John's wort, cinquefoil and wood anemone. A stand of gray twig dogwood grabs your attention either in bloom or when its steel-blue fruit, capping 4-inch corymbs stands forth. At the bottom of the valley, the trail forks. To continue this walk, bear left. (The right fork leads to a parking area on Lodi-Springfield Road.)

You'll climb again. Just before you re-enter the woods, there's a great view to the west. The creek and County Y beyond snake through the valley below you. This valley was undoubtedly changed by the glacier. Instead of being sharply V-shaped, like valleys in the unglaciated areas west of here, it is more U-shaped. It's possible that a giant hunk of ice sat down in the valley for some time after the bulk of the glacier retreated north. Sediment from the iceburg settled out as the ice melted and softened the curvature of the valley.

For the next .2 miles, the trail is in woods, descends into that valley, and to a parking lot on Lodi-Springfield Road. To return to your car, turn around and retrace your steps to the trailhead. ▲

Pothole Trail
Interstate Park

*A short trek leads to a spectacular gorge and
ancient potholes cut by glacial meltwater.*

Distance: One-half mile.

Time: One-half to one hour.

Path: Well-worn and easy to follow, with natural rock steps. There are few signs, but the trail is obvious.

Directions: From the intersection of Highway 8 and Highway 87 just south of St. Croix Falls, take Highway 8 east to Highway 35. Turn south on Highway 35; the park entrance is one-half mile down the road, on the right. A state park sticker is required.

Contact: Interstate Park
Highway 35, Box 703, St. Croix Falls, WI 54024; (715) 483-3747.

At Interstate Park, nature has made unique and interesting creations from her very own rock, creations that have attracted tourists for more than a hundred years. In fact, local citizens so valued the scenery here that, at the turn of the century, they influenced the Wisconsin and Minnesota governments to form the park—the nation's first such "interstate" effort. This was also the first of Wisconsin's state parks.

Interstate now has more than nine miles of walking trails. The Pothole Trail allows you to sample some spectacular views and witness the results of interesting geological processes. Rocks here were formed from molten lava that spewed from the earth a billion years ago. Meltwater from glaciers that arrived much later, along with the water of the St. Croix River, cut the park's centerpiece: a spectacular gorge known as the Dalles of the St. Croix.

Start this walk from the Pothole Trail parking lot about three-quarters of a mile into the park. This is a loop trail and you are going to walk it counterclockwise, so bear right when the trail splits. You'll walk through scrubby oak and pine woods for a few minutes until you hear the sound of the river. Through the trees, you'll be able to see

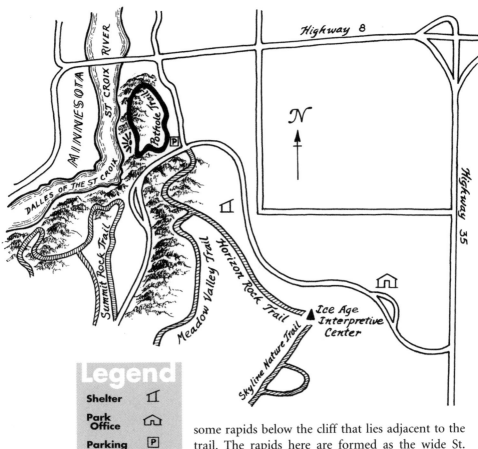

Legend

Shelter	🏛
Park Office	🏠
Parking	Ⓟ
View	☀
Trail	▬
Intersecting Trail	▨

some rapids below the cliff that lies adjacent to the trail. The rapids here are formed as the wide St. Croix squeezes into an ancient rock fault. There are several trails leading off to the right that provide a good view of 2-foot-high standing waves and even bigger rollers churning 80 feet below you. One eddy on the other side of the river, just downstream from the beginning of the rapids, looks big enough to swallow a canoe and not spit it out until the St. Croix's confluence with the Mississippi.

Back on the trail, you'll know you're near the trail's namesakes when you reach a wooden bridge that spans some great hunks of rock. If you examine the rocks around you, you'll see potholes. These are golfball- to car-sized holes in solid rock. What made them? Geologists tell us that at the time of the most recent glacier, about 15,000 years ago, the entire St. Croix basin that you are now walking through was under water, as ice to the north melted and Glacial Lake Duluth began to overflow. The torrent carried more water than any modern-day river, and was one of the biggest rivers that ever flowed across the face of the earth.

All this water swirling southward carried boulders, sand and gravel along with it. The sand and gravel got trapped in whirlpools and eddies, scoured the hard basalt rock and formed bowl-like depressions. As the process continued, the bowl got deeper, and the eddy got stronger. It could then move even bigger rocks that fell into the current. These big rocks, some the size of bowling balls, ground away at the bottom of the bowls until either the river changed channel or its level dropped. What was left are the potholes that you can see from this vantage point. Across the river in Minnesota, in the other half of Interstate Park, is the world's deepest pothole. It's more than 60 feet deep and 12 to 15 feet wide at the top. The biggest pothole along this trail is located underneath the next wooden bridge, down the trail a bit. This car-sized hole is filled with rocks, silt and other debris, however, so you can't tell how deep it is.

For the next couple of hundred yards, views of the river and the Dalles of the St. Croix are the trail's main attraction. From a number of rock outcroppings, you can see the water 135 feet below you and examine the two rock cliffs through which it passes.

This is a good place to recall the role of the St. Croix River in Wisconsin's lumbering empire. Like other major rivers in northern Wisconsin, it was the conduit down which pine logs were floated from the woods to the mills. Because the St. Croix narrows here at the Dalles, logs would sometimes get clogged up. In June 1886 what may have been the world's largest logjam backed an estimated 160 million board feet of logs three miles upstream. It took 200 men and uncounted sticks of dynamite six weeks to free the logs. White pine was king in those days, and if you look at the cliffs visible from your overlook, you'll see that white pine is regaining its throne.

From here, it's just 150 yards through that scrubby jack pine and oak woods back to the parking area where you began this walk. ▲

31

Upper and Nature Trails
Castle Mound Park
Black River Falls State Forest

*A challenging scramble to castellated rock formations
and a view of the site of Glacial Lake Wisconsin.*

Distance: Three miles.

Time: Two hours.

Path: A worn footpath, usually rocky. There are some signs, but the trail on the bluff is not marked well and you have to find your own way down off the bluff. The terrain is hilly.

Directions: From the intersection of Highway 27 and Highway 12 south of Black River Falls, take Highway 12 east 3/4 mile to the park entrance. The parking area is off the park road just beyond the DNR visitor contact station. A state park sticker is required.

Contact: Wisconsin Department of Natural Resources
910 Highway 54E, Black River Falls, WI 54615; (715) 284-1400.

From the east end of the parking lot, start your walk on the nature trail that circles Castle Mound. You'll see big white pine: some of the largest in the southern half of the state. Then you'll see rocks the size of fishing boats. Go past the intersection where the nature trail comes in on the left till you reach a sign that says "overlook." Then bear left and begin your climb up onto the mound, walking on a soft carpet of red oak leaves and pine needles.

Castle Mound is one of a few such mounds scattered around Jackson and Clark counties. Half a billion years ago, a giant inland sea covered this area of Wisconsin and laid down thick layers of sand, which hardened into sandstone. Over the eons since, erosion has erased much of the sandstone. Left in place, however, are the layers that contain pieces of extremely hard quartz, which were cemented into the mix as the sandstone formed. As you walk, notice how these millions of quartz specks make the rock on the mound dance and sparkle with reflected sunlight.

The trail soon passes a long, horizontal rock outcrop on the left. The outcrop is 40 feet tall, tan in color and decidedly layered, looking like slightly melted alternating layers of mocha and cinnamon ice cream piled upon one another. The trail curves left around the east end of this pile of ice cream, and you can get a good look at its east face and north side. This and the rest of the rock up on the top of the mound are exposed Cambrian sandstone.

As the trail continues, there are several side trails that head down the hillside to the mound-circling nature trail. Ignore them. You want to continue up the mound on some wood steps to a plateau where you'll pass big rectangular clumps of rock. Then you'll be at the entrance to the "castle." Gigantic house-sized rocks line the trail on both sides. A 40-foot-tall rock parapet rises to your left, its Stonehengelike rock slabs reaching to the sky. The south face of this rock cliff is smeared with chartreuse-colored moss that looks like ancient cave art.

Then it's time to climb. A couple of wood steps lead up, into and through the rock wall to your left. Six more steps draw you around to the north side of the wall. Twenty-five steps take you to the top of the rock. A four-step steel ladder brings you to a concrete landing poured between rock monoliths. Be careful as you climb these stairs; their iron I-beams can crease your skull.

The landing was built by prisoners from a work camp near Black River Falls in the early 1960s. Originally a fire lookout, the perch now gives ambitious walkers a view of the great Central Plain, part of old Glacial Lake Wisconsin. Fifteen thousand years ago, as the Wisconsin glacier slowly melted, this wide, flat area to the south and east was covered with a gigantic lake. Water escaping from the lake further sculpted the land- scape you see

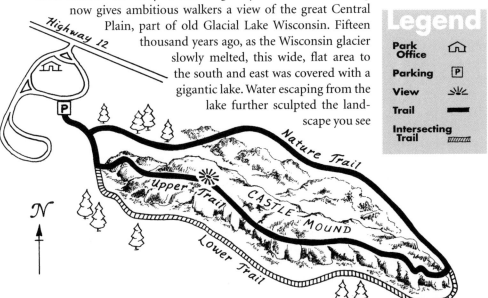

Legend

Park Office ⌂

Parking P

View ☀

Trail ▬

Intersecting Trail ▥

now through erosion and sand deposition. The unglaciated "driftless area" is clearly visible as a line of hills starting off to the northwest and wrapping around to the south.

Your walk takes you back down the stairs and along the north face of the mound for 50 feet or so until the trail cuts back through the Stonehenge rock to the south side of the mound. The trail here is indistinct and you must pick your way between and over chunks of rock. There are several rock-tops that offer partial views off to the south. It's not carefree walking. The trail traverses the high point or "spine" of the mound and at times you'll be close to a precipice with a 30- to 50- foot drop.

Eventually you'll reach a gap in the rock spine that's 10 yards wide. To cross it, you will need to descend from the spine and then climb back up again. So backtrack about 50 feet till you come to a place where you'll be able to climb down the north side of the rock spine. When you get to the bottom of the gap, look south through it, and you can see a big chunk of rock that used to be part of the spine. It came loose, tumbled down the hillside, and sits forlornly out of place.

Just past the gap, you'll climb back up on top of the spine of rock and enter an area of stark stone outcrops. Vertical rock pinnacles point 40 and 50 feet into the air. Big old pine snags stand along the trail, bleached by years of sun. Rotting pine trunks lie fallen in a jumbled mess down the hillside. It's evident there was a disaster of some kind here. Can you guess? No, it wasn't a windstorm, nor did insects kill these trees. In April 1977 fire swept through the Brockway area south of Black River Falls. It charged all the way up the east end of Castle Mound and the trees you see scattered about were killed during that fire.

The trail crests the fire-stripped rock face. Graffiti vie with moss for space on the rock surface. The route off the mound begins just north of a little grassy area atop the bluff. It's long and steep: From the top, a baseball-sized rock, inadvertently kicked off its perch, bounces down the hillside for eight seconds. Use saplings for handholds as you descend.

The nature trail, which you join, is wide and unmistakable here. When you reach it, head left. This north side of the mound is noted for its microclimate. You'll suddenly be walking in a forest much like the one you find in northern Wisconsin, with sugar maples and white pine above your head and partridgeberry and bunchberry beneath your feet. There are also some house-sized rocks that fell off the mound and came to rest on the plain below, amid big white pine. Enjoy the half mile or so walk back to the parking area. ▲

Walks With a View

32

Brady's Bluff West Hiking Trail
Perrot State Park

A short, steep walk leads to the state's best view
of the Mississippi River Valley and a lush prairie.

Distance: 1.3 miles up and back on the same trail.

Time: One to two hours, longer if you become intoxicated with the view.

Path: The terrain is very hilly. It is well-maintained and easy to follow. Signs mark trailheads and key intersections.

Directions: From the intersection of Highway 35 and Main Street in Trempealeau, go south on main street and turn right at the river onto First Street. First Street takes you into the park. Park in the lot that is about a hundred feet past the boat landing, on the left. A state park sticker is required.

Contact: Perrot State Park
Route 1, P.O. Box 407, Trempealeau, WI 54661; (608) 534-6409.

The top of Brady's Bluff offers perhaps the best view of the Mississippi River Valley north of Wyalusing. There are also some exceptional trees, a maidenhair fern-covered hillside and native prairie remnants along this walk.

The trailhead is located across the park road from the parking area. It is marked with a sign, "Brady's Bluff, West Walking Trail." The trees here are wonderful. They embrace you the minute you enter the trail from the road. Oak and hickory, walnut and ash, elm and basswood. Both their diversity and their size are impressive.

You'll begin climbing almost immediately, following a ravine. The ravine is the result of erosion, more recent than the formation of the vast system of ridges and coulees that crease the driftless area. Because the ravine is relatively young, it looks jumbled, a little unkempt, with downed trees, exposed roots, raw soil and naked sandstone.

About halfway up the ravine, a black ash that's 9 feet in circumference towers to the left of the trail. Its light-colored trunk stands out in an area where other trees have fallen, or at least not prospered. Another big old ash lies alongside the trail, having succumbed to erosion.

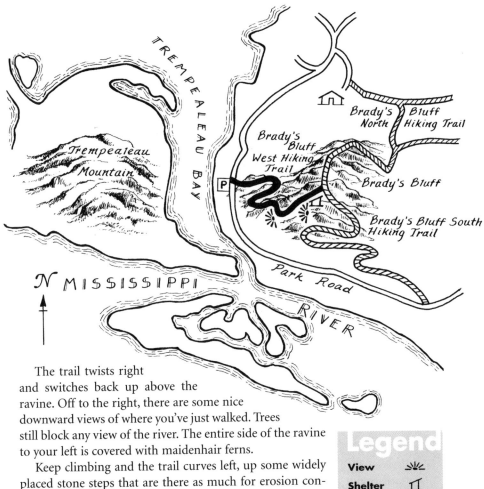

The trail twists right
and switches back up above the
ravine. Off to the right, there are some nice
downward views of where you've just walked. Trees
still block any view of the river. The entire side of the ravine
to your left is covered with maidenhair ferns.

Keep climbing and the trail curves left, up some widely
placed stone steps that are there as much for erosion control as to help you walk. Toward the top of these steps, the
trees thin out and change types. Juniper begin to dominate.
As you climb a set of stairs, you can reach out and touch the
tops of a couple of them. In the fall they often bear lovely
dark, bloomy, blue berries, which when crushed exude a
ginlike fragrance. It's also from the landing on these stairs
that you'll get your first look at the Mississippi River Valley.

Don't dawdle too long because the view is even better farther up
on the bluff. As you exit the initial set of stairs, you'll note that the hillside has been cleared of most trees so that you can see more clearly.
One more set of stairs awaits you before you reach the summit.

At 520 feet high, Brady's Bluff is taller than anything around. Your
view upriver includes, across the river, the city of Winona, Minnesota,

and, on this side, the Trempealeau River bottoms. Directly upriver is Trempealeau Mountain, a striking cone-shaped bump between the river and a vast area of wetlands to its north. Downriver you can see the gap in the bluffs that flank the Mississippi where the Black River cuts through and creates a wetland. Sunset can be remarkable here, as can sunrise, with first sunlight bouncing off the Minnesota bluffs.

You have three options for the walk back down. The first is to return the way you came. The second is to follow the Brady's Bluff North Walking Trail, which heads north off the bluff. This route affords a view of one of the neatest prairie remnants in the park. Following it, you will come to a large meadow that stretches out below you. In the fall, the tall Indian grass, dotted with a few light-blue asters and plenty of yellow goldenrod, is breathtaking. This trail ends at the park office. From there you must walk along the park road for about .6 miles to get back to your car. The third option is to follow the Brady's Bluff South Walking Trail, which winds down the southeast side of the bluff, giving you a couple of views down the river and ending at the park road. Turn right here, and walk about a third of a mile along the road to reach the parking area where you left your car. ▲

33

Buena Vista Trail
City of Alma

Watch river travel creep up the broad Mississippi from a superb perch high above the city of Alma.

Distance: 1.5 miles round trip.

Time: One to two hours.

Path: Generally a very smooth walking surface of mowed grass and dirt. Even though the grade is continuous to the top, the walk is surprisingly easy. There's a small "Walking Trail" sign posted on a power pole near the start, but that is it for signs. Once you're on the trail it would be almost impossible to get lost.

Directions: From Lock and Dam #4 along Highway 35 in Alma, go one block south to Cedar Street. Turn left and go up the steep hill. Turn right onto Second Street and climb up another steep hill. Park anywhere here. The walk begins at the corner of Second and Elm, which is the next street south.

Contact: Alma City Clerk's Office
P.O. Box 277, Alma, WI 54610; (608) 685-3330.

Before you head east up Elm Street to the trailhead, walk to the west side of Second Street and take a look down. Those hills you drove up were indeed steep. Now turn around and look east, up at the blufftop, 500 feet high, that you'll be climbing onto. It's a daunting view.

Walk up Elm Street to its intersection with another blacktop road. The power pole has a small sign posted on it that says "Walking Trail" and points to the left. Proceed, but notice the reddish-orange brick house on your left. It was built in 1904 by a local merchant. Many of Alma's buildings are historically significant. If you are interested in such things, get the brochure titled "Alma's Historic Tour Guide" and walk or drive through town.

The blacktop ends after one block, and the path turns into a wide, mowed grassy one. It curves right, up the hill. This first section of trail is the steepest, so if you're sucking a bit of air here, don't worry, things get easier. Note the eroding hillside on the right. Birch cling precariously to bare dirt. The first of several deep ravines yawns off to your left. The trail makes a 90-degree right turn; a large old black walnut tree marks the inside corner. There are a lot of big and small dead elm along the trail. Morel mushroom hunters, who like to search under such trees, probably scour this place in spring.

The trail switches back and forth, climbing the hill by bits and pieces. At one of the first switchbacks, a couple of old eastern poplar have been felled by a storm and diced up by trail cleansers with chain saws. One 2-foot diameter butt log tallies 79 growth rings. Three of their brethren still stand high over the hillside. What a view they enjoy.

About a hundred feet beyond the poplar, the road splits. Take a brief detour to the right if you want to see the Alma city reservoir. This giant concrete cylinder still supplies the city with drinking water. Stand on top and you can see upriver and some of the Minnesota bluffs.

You'll encounter more switchbacks as you continue your walk to the top. Don't try to cut up and across in order to shorten the walk. The hillside is too steep, plus some of the understory plants are prickly ash, a lovely but thorny little tree that will pierce your flesh. If that weren't enough, thorny native barberry also populate the slope.

At one of the switchbacks, a small opening in the canopy greets you. There's a sandstone cliff face, carved with hundreds of messages. One of the rocks makes a wonderful seat. Wildflowers bloom along the path, and, depending on the season, you may see black-eyed Susan, bluebells, woodland sunflower or bergamot. A Virginia juniper clings to the top of the bare cliff, its roots like knees pressing against the soft stone, as it prays against the day it will tumble riverward.

After the sandstone cliffs, the trail narrows a bit, but it's still wide enough for a wagon or car. There's a several-hundred-foot-long straight stretch with a deep ravine on the left, and some views of the river that same direction. When you reach a small washout on the left side of the trail, you're almost to the top. Look up the gully. You can see an old erosion control structure, built out of 3-foot iron pipe. There are several of these farther up along the trail in areas of washouts.

You will exit the woods into an amphitheaterlike bowl, its sloped sides dotted with big oak trees. This is Buena Vista City Park. Bear right and climb up the side of the bowl. On its top there is a stone path that leads farther right to an overlook.

Alma lies beneath you. If you parked your vehicle on Second Street you can probably see it. It seems like you could toss a stone down and hit it. Highway 35 stretches south and around a curve, behind a bluff, past the Dairyland Power Plant. Lock and Dam #4 reaches across the

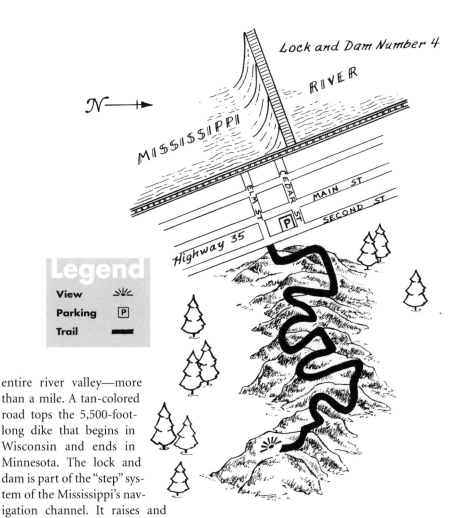

entire river valley—more than a mile. A tan-colored road tops the 5,500-foot-long dike that begins in Wisconsin and ends in Minnesota. The lock and dam is part of the "step" system of the Mississippi's navigation channel. It raises and lowers river traffic seven feet. If you watch the river for long enough, you will see one of the barges, actually several barges strung together, pushed by a river tug. Maneuvering the long rafts into the lock, amid the river current, is a task for a skilled pilot.

Above the dike lies a lake, with islands that look tropical under a summer sun. Elm trees masquerade as palms, canted capriciously, leisurely to this side or that. Below the dike is a wide river and hundreds of channels carving up a rich and diverse bottomland forest of silver and red maple, hickory, elm, basswood and hackberry.

When you have had your fill of the view, retrace your steps back down to your car. ▲

34
Lapham Peak Trails
Lapham Peak Unit
Kettle Moraine State Forest

*Start with a panorama of southeastern Wisconsin
and end with a rambling woods walk.*

Distance: 3.5 miles.

Time: Two to three hours.

Path: Different sections are smooth dirt (or slippery mud in spring and after a rainfall), rocky dirt, mulch-covered dirt or mowed grass. The Ice Age Trail section of the walk is marked with yellow blazes. The park trail is marked as a cross-country ski trail. The terrain includes quite a bit of elevation change.

Directions: From the I-94 and County C interchange, take County C south .9 mile. The park entrance is on the left. Follow the park road to the parking lot by the tower. A state park sticker is required.

Contact: Lapham Peak Unit, Kettle Moraine State Forest
W329N846 County C, Delafield, WI 53018; (414) 646-3025.

Named for Increase A. Lapham (who is considered the father of the U.S. Weather Bureau and collected weather data here), Lapham Peak is the highest point in Waukesha County at 1,233 feet. You will begin this walk from the top of the peak. Trees obscure your view from the ground, but a walk up the tower fixes that. Look east and, on a clear day, you can see the taller buildings of downtown Milwaukee. Lake Michigan is out there too, but it blends in too much with the sky to discern. To the north are little bumps that mark the Northern Kettle Moraine State Forest. On top of one of these sit the quite visible spires of Holy Hill. Closer, to the northwest and to the south, the hills of the Southern Kettle Moraine State Forest undulate to the horizon.

Look for the Ice Age Trail markers that begin to the east of the tower, at the edge of the woods. Descend the 105 steps toward them. You're going to follow the Ice Age Trail to the park boundary to see an old bur oak. Go straight at the first intersection, following the yellow

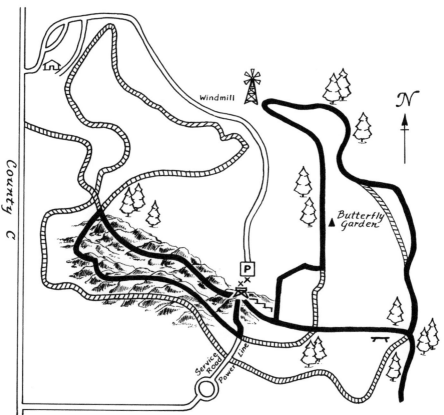

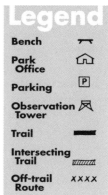

Ice Age Trail blazes as they take you farther downhill. At the next intersection, this time a junction with the cross-country ski trail system, make a 20-foot jog to the right along this ski trail, and you will see the Ice Age Trail continue on down the hill. The trail changes some, becoming narrower and more strewn with rocks. The trees are also smaller here, and the understory thicker.

When you reach a clearing with a bench, it's only about 100 feet farther to the park boundary. Just before reaching the boundary, note the enormous bur oak on the left. This venerable old giant is dying, trunk scarred by past logging and limbs probably affected by chestnut borer. It's still a tree worth hugging.

Retrace your path back up the hill to the ski trail. Turn right and soon you'll be out of the woods, into a large opening. The open expanse and brightness is welcome after walking under a dark canopy. When the mowed path splits, take the right branch, back into the woods. After a dip down a small hill, you'll see a small, half-acre opening on the right. Notice the trees bordering it. Their fernlike appearance, along with the compound leaves with 10 or 12 leaflets, tell you these are walnuts. They have been planted here, as a sort of border to a conifer plantation.

The wide ski trail will take you into another clearing, then back into the woods, along a ridge and into Homestead Hollow, where settlers lived almost a century ago. A scaffold for an old windmill is visible off to the right. Several mowed paths cross in Homestead Hollow; follow the ski trail signs and they will lead you up a gradual but long hill (nicknamed "Asthma Hill" by cross-country skiers). Back in the woods, you'll walk down a long, straight segment of trail that's obviously an old road. Big oaks and one large black cherry line the left side of the road.

At the first opening to the left, near a bench, there's a fenced butterfly garden. Depending on the season, you may see butterfly weed, asters, goldenrod, coneflower, blazing star or a host of other wildflowers that attract butterflies. A sign carries this quote, "The butterfly counts not months but moments, and has time enough."

The lovely treelined country lane ends at a Y junction where you go right and follow signs to the tower. It's a couple hundred yards to the steps that marked the beginning of your walk.

Once back at the tower, if you feel like making another loop down and up the hill, contine west, past the drinking fountain, across a paved service road, and into a picnic area. Look for the Ice Age Trail post and sign along the wood's edge. There are no steps here, just a steep dirt path. In the middle section of your descent off the peak you will notice that you're walking through a wonderful grove of white and red oak. Look up at them. Their angles and diagonals are captivating. Some are straight. Some curve, gently arching across the sky, forming tangents with other trunks and limbs. They dance together in stillness, a century-long ballet, noticed only by a few walkers.

You will know you're at the bottom of the hill when you reach another wide, mowed trail, with lights on posts. This is the lighted "Green" segment of the cross-county ski trail. Go left a couple hundred feet until you see a bench. The trail forks here and you want to take the left fork. You'll know you've got it right when the trail starts an uphill climb. Start climbing. If you golf, this trail will remind you of your favorite dogleg left, only instead of 450 yards and flat, this one is 850 yards and seriously uphill. This is actually one of the longest and steepest downhill cross-country runs in the state. When you reach the service road and power line, turn left and you'll walk right into the parking lot. ▲

35

Red, Blue and Green Trails
Rib Mountain State Park

Follow rolling terrain for
sweeping views of central Wisconsin.

Distance: Three miles.

Time: One and a half to two hours.

Path: The path is rocky and sometimes full of roots. In the fall, add a wet, slippery layer of newly fallen leaves, and you have a path that is both tricky to walk upon and sometimes difficult to see. Trailheads are not marked well; it can take an act of faith to head off down the trail on the assumption that you've chosen the correct way. The trails themselves are marked with blazes, colored leaf stencils, wood posts (sometimes hard to see) and little round metal tags. The terrain playfully dips and rises, never becoming too taxing.

Directions: From the Highway 51 and County N interchange, go west on County N .3 mile to Park Road. Turn right and climb 1.7 miles to the park contact station. A state park sticker is required.

Contact: Rib Mountain State Park
5301 Rib Mountain Drive, Wausau, WI 54401: (715) 842-2522.

This walk is best when there are no leaves on the trees. The view of central Wisconsin from the observation tower and several other points along the trail is outstanding even with leaves on the trees, but without them you get a better overall sense of the mountain. The massive rocks are also more visible after leaf-drop—there are a couple of balancing types here that would be major tourist attractions if they were located in Wisconsin Dells.

Start your walk from the observation deck near the top and on the north side of the hill. There is no trailhead sign, but the stairs leading off from the bottom of the deck are easy to see. While the newer, wider and well-mulched four-mile-long Yellow Trail affords the most hill climbing, it traverses the south side of the mountain, staying mostly in the trees. This walk will follow the older Green, Red and Blue Trails, which stay up near the top of the mountain. They offer the best views and go by some neat rock formations. You will join the Red

Trail in less than 30 feet. Turn left onto it.

One of the first things you'll notice on this walk are the rocks: hundreds, thousands of blue-gray rocks strewn about the hillside. Unlike most of the rocks you'll see while walking the Ice Age or North Country trails, these rocks didn't roll here, nor were they carried. They have lived here their entire 1.7-billion-year life. They are the mountain. Some are not mere rocks at all, but are part of the bedrock, connected to a hunk of quartzite rock that reaches down over a thousand feet.

Many of the rocks on the north side of the hill, uphill from where you are walking, are decorated with moss and lichen. The blue-gray rock blends beautifully with the drab olive of the lichen and the dark but soft green of the moss. Add small, white-barked birch trees as a vertical background and the scene is incredible.

As you're admiring the mix of inanimate rocks and living plants, your attention will be drawn to the first overlook. A bare rock outcrop serves as a viewing platform. Below you stretches the Rib River, its route indicated by an unbroken, elongated patch of trees from west to east, with occasionally visible water. On a very clear day you can see the rough outline of the Harrison Hills on the horizon. Even more rarely, you can see Lookout Mountain.

Not far from the overlook is another mass of stone and plants. Polypod ferns cascade over the rocks, the whole appearing to be tumbling off the side of the mountain.

As the trail begins its twist to the south, across the top of the west side of the hill, note the rampartlike rock formation on your left. This battlement has fought off thousands of years of wind and water.

Once you begin walking back to the east, watch for a tricky trail mark. The blazes on the trees go from red to green for no apparent reason. Trust the path and continue. You will have reached the Green Trail when you can see an observation deck. When you reach an intersection, you'll want to continue on the Red, turning right, away from the deck.

The trail leads mildly downhill to another overlook, this one facing south. Both Mosinee Hill, to the left, and Hardwood Hill, to the right, bump up off the landscape around them. A much smaller bump sits on the horizon to the southwest. That's Power's Bluff, in Wood County.

The trail traces the hillside for a while and then climbs upward, past some talus on the left that has tumbled down from old cliff walls above. The junction with the Yellow Trail is obvious, Yellow being a wide, mulched affair on which people snowshoe in the winter. Turn

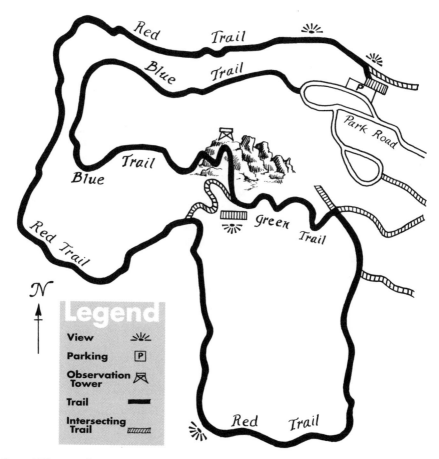

Legend

View	☀
Parking	P
Observation Tower	🏯
Trail	▬
Intersecting Trail	▨

left on Yellow and go up it about 150 feet to where a red oak tree grows in the middle of the trail. If you look to either side of the trail you will see a path that crosses the Yellow Trail here. Turn left and you are on the Green Trail. Relatively flat, it will lead you past another viewpoint, this one to the south, and then on to an observation deck.

The view from the deck isn't as good as the other two south-facing views you've had, so trot past the deck on toward the observation tower. On your way you'll pass a sign that tells you about quartzite, the unusually hard mineral that composes most of the Rib Mountain rock. You'll also pass a sign that points out one of the highest spots in the state, a jumble of rocks that rises 25 feet off the flat to a height of 1,940 feet.

After a 100-step climb to the top of the tower, you have the best view in all directions. About the only direction you haven't seen so far is east, and, save for a few compass degrees that are blocked by tall trees, you can see east from here: the Wisconsin River Valley and Lake Wausau, a lake created by a dam at the Rothschild paper plant. The size and sprawling nature of the lake surprises even locals.

To finish this walk, descend the tower and head southwest toward a blue blaze on a tree. When you get to the tree, climb up onto the rocks next to it and you will see more blue blazes ahead. Don't follow the bare dirt path to the right; it's a short-cut across the mountain top. Follow the blue blazes and you will be on the Blue Trail, which loops about half a mile out to the west edge of the mountain top. The trail is essentially viewless, but interesting because most of it climbs over the top of rock outcrops, with lots of steps: three up, five down, six up and so forth. When you reach the outcrop on the north side of the mountain, take one last view north, then climb a few more rock steps to a wall of rock upon which balances a 50-ton obelisk. The formation is a wonder, worthy of praise.

The end of your walk is just ahead. Stay with the blue blazes and you soon will see the parking area at the north observation deck. ▲

St. Peter's Dome and Morgan Falls Trail
Chequamegon National Forest

Combine a difficult climb to a great northern vista with an easy stroll to a waterfall.

Distance: Three miles round trip to St. Peter's Dome; one mile round trip to Morgan Falls.

Time: Three to four hours.

Path: The trek to St. Peter's Dome is a very difficult uphill climb on a rock- and root-infested trail that is pretty much as God and thousands of walkers have left it. Signage is inconsistent. Be alert to the path, and if you lose it, backtrack. One could get very lost here. A side trip to Morgan Falls is inconsistently marked with blue blazes, but the path is well-worn.

Directions: The trail is hard to find so it's a good idea to refer to the *Wisconsin Atlas & Gazetteer* or some other detailed map. From the third intersection of County C and Highway 13 approximately 10 miles north of Mellen, take County C west and south about 7.5 miles. When County C turns north, continue west instead on Feeney Road for 1.5 miles until Feeney makes a T intersection with County Line Road (Forest Road 199). Turn left (south) on County Line and, in 2.3 miles, you will see the parking area on the left, just south of where the road crosses Morgan Creek.

Contact: Glidden Ranger Station, USDA Forest Service Box 126, Glidden, WI 54527; (715) 264-5701.

This is the kind of trail that demands your attention. Sightseeing and walking are two separate activities here; you can't look around and safely place your foot at the same time. Eye-foot coordination is imperative! Even the best of walkers will catch a toe once or twice on the long pull up to the dome. But the effort is worth it for the view from the top.

You will be walking in what is known as the Penokee Range, which was created more than a million years ago. Once as dramatic as the Alps, the Penokees were reshaped during four glacial periods. Today, they mark the point that separates the watersheds that flow north to Lake Superior from those that flow south to the Mississippi River. St. Peter's Dome is a red granite summit about 1,600 feet high.

This area, and much of the Penokee Range, has seen mining activity. Most of the rock is red granite. Silver was found in the 19th century, but not in abundance. Early in the 20th century a mineral called black gabbro, or black granite, was discovered. An excellent rock for monuments and building stone, it is found only in two regions in the world: the Swiss Alps and here.

Start your walk from the parking area. A sign at the beginning of the route tells you it's 1.5 miles to the dome. You'll immediately cross a small bridge that spans a verdant, fern-covered area with an intermittent stream.

After walking about two-tenths of a mile through typical Wisconsin third-growth timber, you'll reach Morgan Creek. Note that the trail to Morgan Falls goes right—you'll explore it later on your return trip. For now, you'll need to cross the creek, which doesn't have a bridge. Note the yellow-birch limb reaching out over the creek bed. Its smooth, worn bark tells you that folks have used it as a walkway. There are also lots of other log/rock combinations that let you step dry-footed to the other side.

The wide gravel trail continues past the creek, climbing gradually. Soon you'll note water trickling down the trail. It comes from an artesian well a few yards away. The water seeps out from the old, round cistern made of native stone that surrounds it. If you test the water, you'll note its cool, springlike nature. But don't drink it without treating or boiling it first. Giardia are wild and natural too, and will give you quite a stomachache.

Continuing on the path, you'll walk along a little creek bed through a fen. Down a steep slope to the left is Long Lake. There's a car-sized rock on the left also, along with some of the largest false solomon seal you'll ever see growing.

Soon you'll be heading downhill. The loss of altitude is disconcerting since there is a big climb ahead, but it is rewarding. You'll hear the soothing gurgling of water spilling over rock. The trail gets darker and darker due to large hemlocks and cedars that shade the draw you've entered. You'll rock-hop across a small brook, then tango with tangled roots as you climb out of the draw and away from the brook. (It's worth noting that on the return walk this brook crossing is not evident. Many people have missed a slight left turn and continued on along the back of the brook; in other words, the wrong path is more apparent than the rock-hop over the brook. Note a landmark for

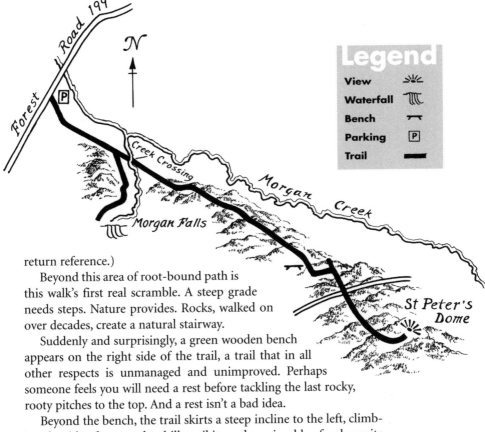

return reference.)

Beyond this area of root-bound path is this walk's first real scramble. A steep grade needs steps. Nature provides. Rocks, walked on over decades, create a natural stairway.

Suddenly and surprisingly, a green wooden bench appears on the right side of the trail, a trail that in all other respects is unmanaged and unimproved. Perhaps someone feels you will need a rest before tackling the last rocky, rooty pitches to the top. And a rest isn't a bad idea.

Beyond the bench, the trail skirts a steep incline to the left, climbing the side of yet another hill until it reaches a jumble of red granite rocks, each bigger than a semitruck tire. Approaching from below, the jumble looks decidedly unnatural. You'll walk briefly with the jumble on your left, then turn left and climb up to a spot where the trail splits. The trail to the dome goes right. But if you take a short side trip to the left, in 100 feet you'll come to the top of the rock jumble you just saw. Inspect some of the boulders and you'll find old drill holes—a clue that these rocks were blasted out by miners.

Retrace your steps to the spot where the trail split, bear left and you're back on the trail to St. Peter's Dome. You'll cross an old road, probably the one used to get equipment up the hill to quarry the granite.

Another steep climb greets you, then a couple of switchbacks that soften the ascent until you reach a headwall of sorts where a bed of granite anchors small trees and brush. You are almost to the top, so though your legs may protest, you will want to gain the 20 vertical feet by scrambling over the rocks and holding onto trees. A small, grassy opening in the woods, the first opening since the parking lot, awaits you at the top of the headwall. There's also a nice granite boulder that invites you to sit down. But since there's no view, and since you're only a hundred yards from your goal, resist.

Reenter the woods and follow the trail as it bears left, and you'll emerge from the tree canopy onto a granite outcrop. Here, the view north and west is unimpeded. On a clear day only the curve of the earth prevents your seeing Duluth. The Bayfield Peninsula, with its gently sloped mountains, stretches to the north and, to the right, Madeline Island lies surrounded by the blue waters of Lake Superior.

Rest a while; enjoy the view. You can explore the top of the dome, but trees block other views. You may notice that sometimes your footfalls on the grass-covered earth ring hollow. Perhaps soil has washed out from between granite chunks, leaving chambers that reverberate.

Remember to watch your step on the way back down, and don't forget about the difficult-to-find brook crossing.

You'll arrive at the trail to Morgan Falls after crossing Morgan Creek. It will be a left turn, and there is a sign indicating the falls are one-half mile away. Morgan Falls is named after a Civil War captain who mined a small amount of silver here in the 1870s. Seventy to 90 feet high (accounts differ), the waterfall is one of the highest in Wisconsin.

The trail hugs the south side of the creek. You will hear the waterfall before you see it. It doesn't roar but fills the high-walled canyon with a higher-pitched sound. Then, suddenly, you are upon the falls, hemmed in on all sides by rock and the vegetation that covers it. A big yellow-birch log serves as a bench. A couple of the log's relatives still stand, shading the canyon floor and its shaggy carpet of interrupted ferns. The waterfall itself is narrow, like a fountain. Could there be a circulating pump hidden somewhere in that mass of rock that pulls the water up to the top ... ?

You can explore the area around the falls, but there is no route up the rock to see the waterfall from a better vantage point—and trying to make one would cause erosion. Better to admire the cascade from below, then retrace your steps to the St. Peter's Dome trail junction. Once there, turn left and you're headed back to the parking lot. ▲

Walks
With a
Goal

37

Across Door County
Waters End Road

*Walk a country road from one side
of Door County to the other.*

Distance: Four miles one way.

Time: One to two hours one way.

Path: Paved town road, with narrow, crushed-limestone shoulders part
of the way.

Directions: This walk is best done with a car shuttle. Leave one car at the end of
your walk, near the breakwater at the eastern terminus of Waters
End Road. To get there, take County ZZ east and north from Sister
Bay until it intersects with Waters End Road; turn right and follow
Waters End Road to its end. Then drive to the beginning of the
walk by retracing your route to Sister Bay. From town, go north on
Highway 42 approximately 1.5 miles to Waters End Road. You can
park a car along the shoulder of Highway 42.

Contact: None. This is not an official walking path.

The Door County countryside, rolling and dotted with orchards,
fields, pastures, upland woodlots, old farmsteads and cedar
swales, is the epitome of pastoral. By walking along Waters End
Road, you can begin with your feet in the waters of Green Bay and finish with them in the waters of Lake Michigan—and you do so by traveling a straight line of only four miles!

Start the walk on the beach directly west of the western end of
Waters End Road. The sun will be at your back and the soles of your
boots immersed in Green Bay. The view west is great. To the northwest, the Sister Islands poke out of the bay. Southwest, the bluffs of
Peninsula State Park jut into the sky. Due west, Sister Shoals peak
above the wave tops.

Waterfront homes hug each side of the road as you head east, up
an incline, making your way to Highway 42. Cross the highway and
more climbing brings you to Hillcrest Road. Take a look back, and
wave goodbye to Green Bay. Ahead is an arrow-straight road, canopied

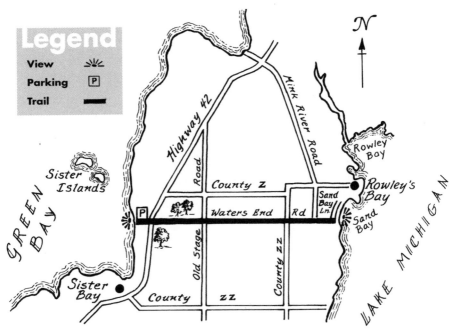

by arching sugar maple branches.

A third of a mile into the walk, a cherry orchard occupies the field to the right. It's surrounded by a high-voltage fence. This discourages deer (and presumably people). Cherries have been a cash crop in Door County for more than a hundred years. The big waters of Green Bay and Lake Michigan stabilize temperatures, preventing late-spring and early-fall frosts that can ruin a crop. Shortly after you pass the orchard, the canopy of sugar maple closes over you. A Door County woodlot stretches away from the road to the north.

Near Wallen Lane you'll find an apple orchard on your left. Most of these trees are Wealthy apples, an old favorite good for cooking, but you'll also see an occasional odd-type apple tree, perhaps planted by mistake. Apple trees do not grow true to type from seed and all the trees you see are the result of grafts. Like cherry trees, apple trees do well in Door County because of the moderated climate.

You'll reach a stand of pole-sized white ash. This is an unusual stand, rare because it's so exclusively white ash—more typically you'll see them in a mix of other trees, such as maple and elm. Perhaps a settler planted these trees, scattering seed in this spot.

At Old Stage Road, notice the white house on your left. It's more than 120 years old, built by an early pioneer. Today it houses Elaine Johnson and Gretchen Johns, current owners of the Northern Lights Fish Co. They buy whitefish from Door County fishermen and proccess them for local sale. Some of that boiled fish you ate last night may have come from here. The cedar-shake shack close to the road once was a haymow, completed in 1885.

Past the homestead, notice the cedar growing on both sides of the road. Usually relegated to wet, swampy places elsewhere in the state, cedar grows like a weed in Door County. Because the deer herd here is small, cedar is not browsed as heavily as in other areas of the state.

You'll pass an old field on your left. Once cultivated, it's been allowed to revert back to its former character. A little farther, neglected orchards occupy both sides of the road. The dead and dying apple and cherry trees are sad testament to the effort needed for successful farming, even in blissful Door County.

In another half-mile or so, you'll reach an active dairy farm. The hayfield supports a herd of approximately 40 cows. Several old farmstead buildings sit in the lot to your right. Notice the hewn-log construction. After that, you'll see a stone fence. The barbed wire that occupies the middle of the stone suggests that wire came first, then the stone was piled along it as the farmer cleared his field. Imagine the effort involved in picking all that dolomite and carrying it to the fence line!

Soon rolling hills appear, dotted with common juniper and undulating off to the horizon. At County ZZ, you'll find an old fur farm, low-slung buildings standing forlornly, on your right. Though this farm did not prosper, Wisconsin produces more ranch mink than any other state—about 700,000 pelts a year.

You'll top a hill—the highest point on your journey. Ahead, a piece of Lake Michigan is visible at the end of the road.

In another half-mile, you'll come upon a cedar woods on your left. This low, boggy area is more typical of "cedar swamps" in the rest of the state.

You'll reach North Sand Bay Lane in a quarter of a mile. Think about taking a side trip down it now or later. In less than half a mile, you'll find Sand Bay Town Park, with pit toilets, swings, grills and picnic tables in a cedar grove, with a sand beach beyond. This little gem of a park is not on most maps.

Shortly after this intersection, land ends. A concrete breakwater extends 200 feet into the lake at Sand Bay, a dimple in the shoreline of the larger Rowley Bay. Gulls greet you, along with the hull of an old fishing scow, high and dry along the road. Still-working fishing boats bob at their moorings along the breakwater. Get your soles wet so you can claim you've traversed the entire peninsula, bay to lake. Not many folks have accomplished such a feat, no pun intended. ▲

38

To Wisconsin's Highest Point
Timm's Hill National Trail

Expect lake views and lots of climbing on your way to the top of Timm's Hill.

Distance: Six miles round trip.

Time: Two to four hours round trip.

Path: Wide, invitingly maintained and well-marked, with red blazes on the trees.

Directions: From the intersection of Highway 13 and Highway 86 just west of Ogema, go east on Highway 86 approximately 4.5 miles to County C. Go right on County C three miles and you will see where the trail crosses the road. Park here on County C. There is a trailhead marker sign on the left side of the road.

Contact: Price County Tourism Department
126 Cherry St., Phillips, WI 54555; (800) 269-4505.

This is a walk to the top of Wisconsin. At 1,952 feet above sea level, Timm's Hill can be viewed as the last glacier's crowning achievement. Having collected soil, rocks and perhaps a woolly mammoth tusk or two on its southerly advance, the glacier melted and left enough debris here to make this Wisconsin's highest point.

Begin next to an old one-room schoolhouse that looks like it's been converted to a residence. Head north down the trail and note the elaborately cut pickets on the old picket fence on the left, which likely was part of the schoolhouse complex. The trees that have grown up next to it are about 40 years old.

You will encounter a wet area in about 50 yards. Stay to one side or the other and you can keep your feet dry. After walking through a clear-cut for about an eighth of a mile, you'll climb a steep hillside up to a meadow. The trail follows the meadow and then curves right along an aspen-covered ridge. There is water down a steep embankment to the left. Beaver have worked this upland aspen stand, which is surprising given the distance to the water.

You'll pass a post with a big red "7" emblazoned on it and then head down a long, steep grade that, in three pitches, takes you to the trickle of water below. The view up the little brook is pretty. There's a good climb on the other side of the brook, and then a right turn. A sign on a tree at the turn says, "4.1 Loop." This is a marker for the cross-country ski trail of which this trail is a part. Zillmer Lake, the first of three lovely little lakes along this trail, appears on the left shortly after the ski loop sign. As you walk through this area you will note several deep glacial potholes that didn't fill with water. Also look up and, if the treetops are leafless, you will see several hills that rise high above the lakes and potholes. The second lake you pass is Otter Lake. It's an easy walk over to the shore where you can note more beaver abuse. The beaver here seem to prefer red maple; you can observe hundreds of 1- to 3-inch saplings that have been chewed off about four inches above the ground. The shore around the lake is ringed mostly by conifers, balsam fir and hemlock, with a few white pine too. It's a very pretty scene. The trail splits between Otter Lake and Reuss Lake. There's a large sign-

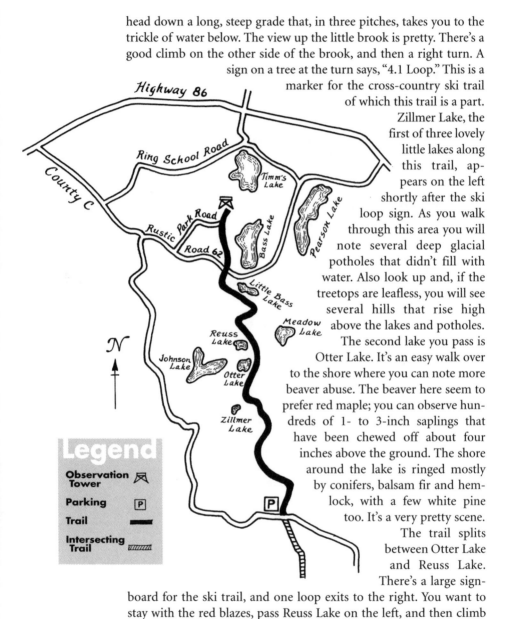

board for the ski trail, and one loop exits to the right. You want to stay with the red blazes, pass Reuss Lake on the left, and then climb up the side of a large hill. Near the top, you will pass another post, this one with a large red "8" on it. A Timm's Hill Trail sign marks another junction and arrows point left. Turn left, again following the red blazes.

Little Bass Lake will soon be on your right side. This is a slightly bigger lake than the first three you've passed. After this lake, you'll walk by a cedar swamp on your left, then a large open marsh, and come to an asphalt road, Rustic Road 62, which you will cross. As you're making the long climb past the road, you'll see Bass Lake on the right. This is the largest lake visible on this walk. When you get to the top of the hill you're climbing, you can look up and slightly to the right and see the outline of Timm's Hill. It looks imposingly high, especially since you have just climbed what felt like a big hill.

After a dip down, you'll reach the Park Road. The trail follows the road around to the parking lot at the base of Timm's Hill. A large sign tells you that the 10-mile path that is Timm's Hill National Trail was the first side trail established under the National Trail System Act. It was constructed by the High Point Ski Club in 1986 and designated in March 1990.

To reach Wisconsin's highest natural point, head toward the sign that says, "Observation Tower." There are some steps and a plaque set in a stone monument that honors the first settlers of Ogema, Spirit and Hill. As you set off up the 300-yard trail that takes you to the summit, consider that the trail you are walking on is the downhill trail for cross-country skiers who venture up to the top. Walking up is easy compared to the tricky descent on skis!

The view from the observation tower is of woodlands stretching off in all directions. A couple of lakes are discernable, as is rolling glacial topography. To return to the road where your car is parked, turn around and retrace your route. ▲

Special Access Trail

Distance: About one-half mile round trip.

Time: Varies with mode of transportation.

Path: The 8-foot-wide surface is relatively flat (no grade exceeds 3 percent) and hard-packed, with limestone screenings to accommodate those with disabilities.

Directions: From the intersection of Highway 13 and Highway 102 west of Rib Lake, go east, through Rib Lake, about seven miles to County C. Turn left on County C and go 2.75 miles to the trailhead parking area on the left. To get here from the trailhead of the walk described above, just continue south on County C about five miles

Contact: Price County Tourism Department
126 Cherry St., Phillips, WI 54555; (800) 269-4505.

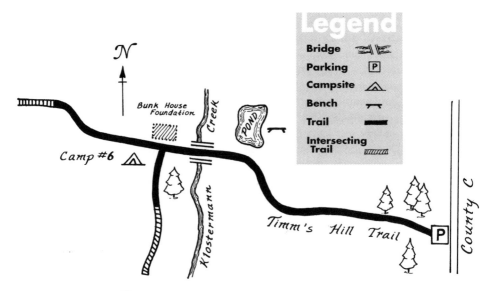

T his trail is the first and, so far, only special-access path on any
National Scenic and Historic Trail in the United States. Its
glacial and historic features make it interesting to anyone.

The trail begins at the south end of the parking area and heads into
a red pine plantation. The area around the plantation must have been
an old gravel pit, as the trail is surrounded by irregular and sometimes
high piles of dirt and gravel. An interpretive sign tells you about the
glacial geography of the area.

There's a manmade pond on the right with a bench overlooking it.
Then a bridge crosses Klostermann Creek. This creek used to be an
old ice road, used in the 1920s for logging operations. There are still
some timbers down in the creek bed, visible off the side of the bridge,
that helped stabilize the creek bed and support the vehicles trans-
porting logs.

Past the creek, you enter the natural woods, composed of oak,
maple, basswood and birch, among other trees. Once you're into this
woods, there's a junction where the Ice Age Trail heads to the left and
Timm's Hill Trail goes straight. Just to the right of the junction is the
site of Camp 6, an old logging camp operated by the Rib Lake Lumber
Company from 1908 to 1911. An old bunkhouse foundation, not easy
to see, sits beneath 90 years of forest decomposition and growth.

The special access trail splits, ending just 50 feet or so down the Ice
Age Trail and continuing for about a hundred feet on Timm's Hill
Trail, until the limestone screenings disappear and the grade steepens.

To return to the parking lot, turn around and retrace your route. ▲

Urban Ambles

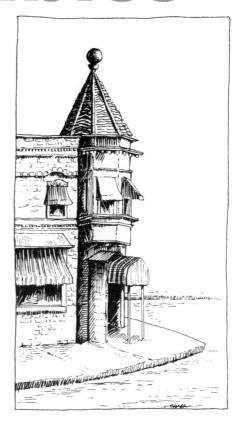

Lake Geneva to Williams Bay Segment
Lake Geneva Shore Path

*Beautiful Victorian mansions line a
unique footpath around Lake Geneva.*

Distance: Seven miles one way.

Time: 2.5 to 4 hours one way.

Path: Fascinating. This is a path that crosses hundreds of private lots. Its existence is protected by law: Landowners along Lake Geneva must allow passage. But the law doesn't say what the path should look like, what it should be made of, how it should be constructed. And without direction, the landowners have created a linear patchwork that's amazing in its diversity. Dirt, lawn, crushed rock of many varieties, paving bricks, regular bricks, concrete, colored concrete stepping stones, aggregated concrete stepping stones, paving bricks sculpted out of concrete, ceramic tiles: The path surface is a potpourri of materials. This trail is essentially unmarked, except for an occasional arrow or detour sign supplied by a considerate construction crew.

Directions: From the intersection of Highway 12 and Highway 50 east of the town of Lake Geneva, take Highway 50 west through the business district to parking areas near the public library. There is metered parking along Highway 50 close to the public beach. Some side streets to the left of Highway 50 are unmetered. It is possible to return from Williams Bay to Lake Geneva by boat. Stop by the Geneva Lake Cruise Line ticket office at the Municipal Dock in Lake Geneva to find out the boat schedule and arrange a pickup. Or you can do your own car shuttle by leaving a second car near Williams Bay Lakefront Park.

Contact: Lake Geneva Chamber of Commerce
201 Wrigley Drive, Lake Geneva, WI 53147; (800) 345-1020.

There are two different kinds of highlights associated with this walk. As with most of the walks in this book, the natural setting is outstanding. The lake is blue and deep and clear. The air has a fresh, marine smell. Lakeside vegetation is lush. But unlike most of the other walks, much of what makes this route outstanding is man-made. The path surface itself is a highlight. The houses and estates along the way amaze. Many date from before the return of the century when prosperous Chicagoans bought property here and built summer homes.

The walk begins at the Lake Geneva Public Library, which is just above the public beach. There is a paved sidewalk between the beach and the library. Head right, counterclockwise around the lake. As you leave the paved walkway and begin walking on the unpaved trail, note the boats moored in the relatively sheltered bay. There are many big boats on Lake Geneva.

The first private pier you pass belongs to the Bosworth family. The Bosworths owned a restaurant in Addison, Ill., and have owned this home for more than 50 years. This out-of-state and prolonged ownership is typical of properties along the lake.

Large size is another attribute of many of the houses along the path, reflecting the affluence of their owners. This is especially true of the older homes. The first tennis court you pass is located on the grounds of one such estate. Maple Lawn was built in 1870-71 by Shelton Sturges, a Chicagoan.

While the large, old houses are impressive, so are some of the bungalows and their attendant gardens. The first time you walk behind a house, note the wonderful garden between the circular drive and the house. If it's spring the magnolia tree may be in bloom.

Besides deciding what kind of path to build, landowners on Lake Geneva must figure out what to do with the lake bank. There are almost as many landscape solutions to this problem as to the path surface. When you see the big white pier with the green-and-white-striped canopy, you are near the daylily solution. Someone has planted hundreds of feet of daylilies along the bank. It's not far to another solution: grass planted beneath willows. These willows are gigantic and reach out gracefully over the water. Note where the trees tipped over into the lake after ice and wave action eroded the bank underneath them. Rather than succumb to this insult, these willows just threw down some roots into the lake and kept growing!

The next very identifiable landmark you'll come to is the Covenant Harbor Bible Camp. Used as a retreat for church groups since 1947, the camp controls several hundred feet of lakeshore. Past the camp buildings you will pass a very odd apple orchard, full of unkempt, crowded little trees. Perhaps someone's attempting to create an apple tree forest.

It's about three-quarters of a mile to one of the more famous

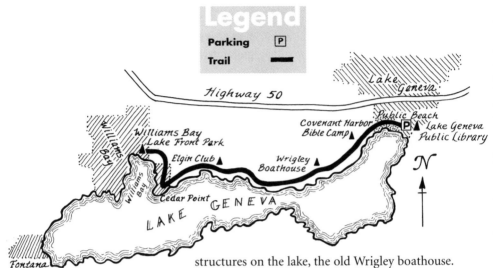

structures on the lake, the old Wrigley boathouse.

Part of a large estate previously owned by the gum magnet, P.J. Wrigley, the boathouse can't be missed, as you will have to step over the old, rusted iron rails leading up to it from the lake. There is a large winch next to the boathouse that was used to pull the ocean-going-sized boats into the house for winter. The darkly stained boathouse is in some disrepair, but has a lot more class than the one constructed of cinder block that you'll pass a little farther down the path.

It's about another quarter mile to Wadsworth Hall, which was built in 1906. This brick and stone mansion with Georgian pillars and multiple brick chimneys is also unmistakable. The grounds are characterized by lawn, then more lawn. A monotonous grass-covered berm keeps the path away from the grounds.

When you reach a chain-link fence and paved road, you are about halfway through this walk. The next architectural wonder is named Glen Fern, built in 1911 for N.C. Sears and made obvious by its granite arches. Even more obvious is the landscaped "creek bed" lavishly paved with stone. Although this is a prodigious piece of landscaping, one wonders where nature disappeared to.

A sign on the path will alert you that you've entered the "Elgin Club," given its name years ago because residents all originated in the Illinois city of Elgin. Homes are close to the lake, their front yards small and tidy. The community may remind you of a residential neighborhood near your home.

After more estates and an area of small, boxlike homes, you'll enter a woods. Uphill, away from the lake, through a natural stand of oak and maple, sits perhaps the most striking home on this entire walk. Its design is Frank Lloyd Wright-like, although he didn't actually participate. The thin, sand-colored stone, laid horizontally, is accentuated by three wide, cream-colored decks, also horizontal in orientation, plus a roof line of similar color and shape. A bold vertical line of windows is planted off-center, the trim colored deep brownish-red. Wow! The landscaping is notable for its simplicity. The trees have been thinned a bit, and the brushy understory removed, except near the property line, where the brush has been left as a buffer. Flagstone steps, laid casually with space between, lead unobtrusively and in a leisurely fashion down to the lake.

You'll soon pass an extensive lawn. It's a combined yard, belonging to at least four different homes. It is seamless, meticulously maintained as one space. Gardens and natural areas border the grass and provide a very pleasant area.

An old flagstone surface marks the beginning of a climb up and over Cedar Point. From the top, you can see the mouth of Williams Bay and the dome of Yerkes Observatory (built in 1897 and the home of the world's largest refracting telescope) on the hill beyond the bay. The path stays on the point's high ground for a while, and folks need stairs to reach their piers. When you do descend off the hill, the houses are all set back from the lake. You'll walk by a couple of private beaches and docks and a couple of small parks. The bay is visible most of the time, and you can't help but notice the eight-story condominiums on the other shore. They don't fit. They're too big.

The path will open into Williams Bay Lakefront Park, a large park with a public boat launching site, city pier, bathhouse and beach. Take a dip if you'd like. Then catch the boat back to Lake Geneva or return via the car you shuttled here. ▲

40

Madison Pub Crawl

Have your drink, your lakes and historic buildings too, on a tavern tour of Wisconsin's capital city.

Distance: 3.5 miles one-way. This walk works best if you arrange a shuttle, leaving one car at the end of the route and taking the other to the beginning.

Time: Two hours or more depending on how much you eat or drink.

Path: Level city sidewalks. We invented this walk so the "trail" is unmarked, but city street signs will help keep you on course.

Directions: Drop off a car near the walk's end point: the University of Wisconsin Memorial Union. (The public parking ramp on Lake Street is a good spot.) Then start your tour at the Harmony Bar and Grill, 2201 Atwood Ave., near the intersection of Atwood Avenue, Eastwood Drive and Dunning Street, approximately 1.5 miles east of the Capitol Square.

Contact: None.

Mad City is notable for its lakes, politics, the university—and bars. As bars go, this walk treats you to variety. From the upscale Edgewater to Mickey's Tavern, you'll sample the best and the basic. Plus, for those who prefer a little nature with their drink, the walk takes you near two lakes, along a river parkway and past the ever-lovely Capitol grounds.

Start at the big and open Harmony Bar and Grill, at 2201 Atwood Ave. Its burgers are famous, as is the blue cheese and chips appetizer. There's a perpetual card game going just inside the front door, and good bands often perform on weekends.

From here, find the blacktop bike path that heads off in a southwesterly direction just west of Dunning Street. You'll get a glimpse of the Barrymore Theatre (originally named the Eastwood Theater) and now a concert hall, located several blocks away on Atwood Avenue. This was the only movie house outside the city center until the 1960s.

The bike path parallels Eastwood Avenue for most of our quarter-mile walk on it. Madisonians take their biking seriously, so you will encounter bikers and roller bladers. Be careful.

The path crosses the Yahara River on a restored bridge. A plaque there reads, "1904 Wisconsin Bridge and Iron Company, Milwaukee, Wisconsin." The river looks inviting, and a green space stretches in both directions. Large tour boats and private craft ply the river.

Mickey's Tavern is located at 1524 Williamson St., just across the bridge. Mickey's is cozy and dark, with lots of wood, giving the place a hollowed-out-log feel. The tavern has been family owned since the early 1900s. The bar, with neon sculptures on the back bar, dates to 1942 and was moved to this location from the Roman End Bar on North Park Street. Check out the "smoked walleye" hanging on the west wall.

From Mickey's, head south down Thornton Avenue, along the Yahara River. You'll pass by Georgia O'Keeffe Middle School, named for the famous artist who grew up in nearby Sun Prairie. This neighborhood, bounded on the east by the Yahara River and on the south by Lake Monona, is known as the Third Lake Ridge Historic District. It's one of Madison's oldest residential neighborhoods and contains houses designed in a rich variety of architectural styles. The blocks bounded by Spaight, Rutledge, Thornton and South Dickenson, for example, contain 47 bungalows built in the 1920s. You can see a sampling of them on your right as you walk down Thornton.

Two blocks south of the school, Morrison Park beckons you to stroll out on the pier and view the Lake Monona shoreline. Follow Morrison Street west, paralleling the lakeshore, for three blocks until Morrison curves right and becomes South Baldwin Street. Note the mix of architectural styles. Varied roof lines and lots of gables are the rule. The Frank and Jeannette Flower house at 706 S. Baldwin has been restored to its original Queen Anne appearance. Look for a wonderful junglelike garden shielding the house on the northwest corner of Jenifer and South Baldwin streets. The limbs of a large black walnut tree reach out and provide a canopy for both jungle and sidewalk.

Your next stop is the Crystal Corner Bar, 1302 Williamson St., at the intersection of Williamson and South Baldwin. The Crystal has a big, island-type bar. A translucent, wavy, glass-block wall lends a beach house feel to the place. Another wall is papered with autographed photos of musicians who have played at the bar during the last 50-plus years. Buddy Guy's picture is here, along with notables like Koko Taylor and Leon Russell. A 25-foot-long, well-filled trophy cabinet attests to the seriousness of bar patrons' sporting interests.

Walk west down Williamson Street through an intriguing neighborhood that mixes storefront shops, restaurants, old factories, upscale residences and human service organizations. You'll pass Jolly

Bob's Jerk Joint, a Jamaican restaurant with an open-air dining area; Steve's Tattoo, with some very interesting designs displayed in the window; Savory Thymes, serving vegetarian cuisine; Broom Street Theater, the oldest year-round experimental theater in the Midwest; Willy Street SRO, a residence for homeless, mentally ill persons; Pet Plus Store, with a giant dog and giant cat atop its roof; Wooden Voices, the home of handmade musical instruments; and a truly odd yard of fences, a display area for the Struck and Irwin Fence Co.

Just past the fence yard, the Livingston Street Power Plant of the Madison Gas and Electric Co. looms large off to the right. The small, white building on the left, a former gas station, has been converted to apartments. Just past the Elks Club you will get your first glimpse of the Capitol dome over the top of other buildings, off to the right.

Jog up Blair Street and across Wilson, and you'll be at your next stop, the Essen Haus, 514 E. Wilson St. Live accordion music strikes your eardrums as you enter, and you're met with the sight of waiters and waitresses dressed in liederhosen. The ceiling is decorated with more than 2,500 beer steins, which belong to faithful patrons. Also referred to as a "Trinken Halle" (drinking hall) in its literature, Essen Haus claims to be "the largest seller of German tap biers in the U.S." Plus it serves 270 bottled imports from around the world. The building is authentic too. It was built in 1863 as the Germania Hotel. Some of the original brick and stone work survives. The cherrywood back bar is from the Fauerbach Brewery, Madison's first brewery, founded in 1848 by Peter Sprecher.

Before you sample too many of those imports, head out the door, and turn right down Wilson Street to King Street. Turn right onto King, and you will see the Capitol building rise before you in all its glory. Turn left at the next intersection, Doty Street, and you will be at the old Fess Hotel (123 E. Doty St.), now the Great Dane Pub and Brewing Co. The building, which was owned by the Fess family for 120 years (until the mid-1970s), is partly constructed of Cream City brick, kilned in Milwaukee. Take a stroll around. There's an outdoor eating and drinking area, shaded with a flowering crab tree, in the back. Downstairs, big copper kettles brew tomorrow's beer behind large glass windows. Try the Dane's "Sampler Pack," a 4- to 9-glass microbrew smorgasbord. As you quaff your beer, remember that Carrie Nation stayed at the Fess in 1901, while campaigning for prohibition. Perhaps she is rolling over in her grave right now!

Continue your walk by heading toward the Capitol on King Street. You'll pass under the marquee for the Majestic Theatre, which caters to an avant-garde crowd with foreign films and off-beat flicks. When

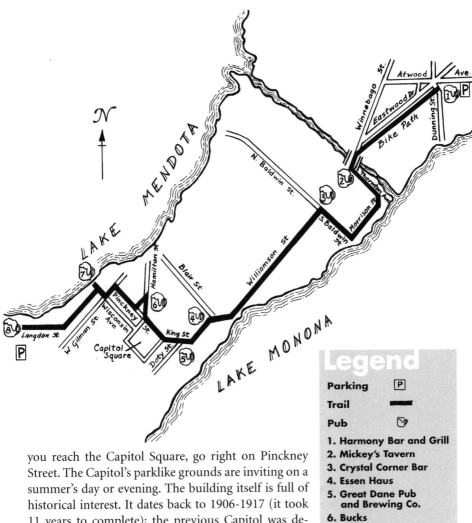

Legend

Parking P

Trail ▬

Pub ☕

1. **Harmony Bar and Grill**
2. **Mickey's Tavern**
3. **Crystal Corner Bar**
4. **Essen Haus**
5. **Great Dane Pub and Brewing Co.**
6. **Bucks**
7. **Edgewater**
8. **University of Wisconsin Memorial Union**

you reach the Capitol Square, go right on Pinckney Street. The Capitol's parklike grounds are inviting on a summer's day or evening. The building itself is full of historical interest. It dates back to 1906-1917 (it took 11 years to complete); the previous Capitol was destroyed by fire in 1904. Look on the very top of the dome and you will see "Forward." She is a gold-leafed sculpture done by Daniel Chester French. He sculpted her on the cliffs of the Hudson River so he could view the piece from the same perspective as from ground level around the Square. Feel free to detour through the building. It's an open and mazelike affair guaranteed to get you confused if you venture off a straight line.

At the northwest corner of the Square, you'll find Hamilton Street. If you want to see one of Madison's most hard-bitten bars, turn onto it and walk (appropriately) past the headquarters of the Wisconsin Tavern League to Bucks (113 N. Hamilton St.), which has a reputation as a place to drink. (Guys, check out the sink in the men's room, built on a cinder-block base. Management must have become fed up with drunks ripping it off the wall, so they made an unassailable shrine to bathroom vandalism.)

Proceed down Hamilton half a block to Dayton Street, then go left one block and you'll be back at Pinckney. Turn right. You have entered the land of the students. You'll recognize it by all the bicycles: on balconies, chained to curbside trees, on porches. Or perhaps you'll hear music blaring from second-story windows or out open doors. From here to the end of this walk, almost a mile, you will pass only one private, single-family home. All the rest are apartments, condominiums, fraternity/sorority houses, bed and breakfasts, hotels and other "commercial" dwellings. What used to be an aggregation of elaborate single-family residences has been turned into housing primarily for students.

On the northwest corner of Pinckney and Gorham streets you will pass Gorham Park. This serene little green space has as its centerpiece one of the state's largest weeping mulberry trees. Take a walk through the area and enjoy its peacefulness.

Just before you reach Gilman Street, you'll find the Mansion Hill Inn (424 N. Pinckney St.), which offers luxury lodging. Also known as the McDonnell-Pierce House, it was built in 1857-58. Alexander McDonnell was the contractor for the second state Capitol, built between 1857 and 1859. He used the same architects for his house as for the Capitol, and they saw fit to use many of the same design elements and the same Prairie du Chien sandstone. The mansion is reputed to be the finest domestic example of German Romanesque Revival architecture remaining in the United States.

Turn left on Gilman and take it one block to Wisconsin Avenue. Turn right onto Wisconsin and follow it past Langdon Street to the Edgewater, where, "The only thing we overlook is beautiful Lake Mendota." While this is a hotel, and an expensive one, it is also an elegant restaurant and fine bar. Whether or not you choose to eat or drink, take the lobby elevator down to lake level and walk out onto the pier. On a summer evening, when the moon is setting to the west, the view is breathtaking, and romantic.

Head west on Langdon. It angles its way past the alpha and omega of Greek fraternity and sorority houses toward your last stop, the University of Wisconsin Memorial Union. If it's warm out, find a seat on the terrace on the lake side of the building and enjoy one more beer. Some nights, great bands play for free. All manner of folks pass by here—it's one of the best people-watching spots in North America. Sit and relax. ▲

41

Milwaukee Tavern Tour

Visit historic pubs while strolling the
neighborhoods of Wisconsin's Brew City.

Distance: About five miles, one way. This walk works best if you arrange a
shuttle, leaving one car at the end of the route and taking the other
to the beginning.

Time: Two to eight hours one way, depending on how much you eat
and drink.

Path: Level city sidewalks. We invented this walk so the "trail" is
unmarked, but city street signs will help keep you on course.

Directions: Leave one car at the end point, near Von Trier, 2235 N. Farwell.
Begin your walk at Gasthaus Zur Krone, which is located two
blocks south of National Avenue at 839 S. 2nd St., near the famous
Allen-Bradley clock tower.

Contact: None.

The highlight of this walk is historic and ethnic Milwaukee. My
friend Rob Speer, a beer aficionado and the architect of this
tour, decided to begin at Gasthaus Zur Krone, which roughly
translates into "Inn of the Crown." Rob says that this tavern has the
best selection of beer in Milwaukee. With 180 different labels and
more on the way, I'd have to agree.

The building dates back to the turn of the century, when it was a
feed and grain store. Its old tin ceiling and plastered walls are ade-
quate enclosure for a German-style bar. The big, poster-sized pictures
of Franz Joseph and other pre-World War I Germans add to the
authenticity of the place.

For serious beer drinkers, there's something called the Meister Bier
Schmeckers Verein ("Beer Tasters Association"). According to an
information sheet supplied by the bar, "This society is open to all true
beer lovers. Its sole purpose is the enjoyment and evaluation of the
great beers of the world. Members are issued cards, mugs and other
awards which will certify to the world their rank in the society." One
hundred and sixty names are engraved on a plaque that hangs on the

wall across from the bar. These are folks who have earned the title "Meister" by quaffing 101 different types of beer.

If you can push yourself away from the bar at Gasthaus Zur Krone, head up north on 2nd Street. Between here and the Milwaukee River you'll be hiking through the Walker's Point Area. It's full of old buildings, some industrial and some abandoned. Cornerstones reveal that several structures date to the late 1800s. If the breeze is onshore, your nose may detect the presence of the Milwaukee filtration plant.

Turn right onto Virginia Street. The buildings on the left are occupied by the Milwaukee Fire Department. The one on the corner of 1st and Virginia has a cornerstone that reads "1900."

Go left (north) on 1st Street. The building now occupied by the Brewmaster Pub and Grill on the west side of 1st was once a brothel. Continue north on 1st Street, and you'll make your first crossing of the Milwaukee River. Looking east from the bridge, you can see tugs berthed along the south shore of the river. On the north shore, an old factory building has been converted to house the Milwaukee Institute of Art and Design. Off in the distance you can see the arches of the famous Hoan Bridge, termed the "Bridge That Goes to Nowhere" after a planned freeway expansion didn't happen.

Coming off the bridge, you'll note an arch with "Historic Third Ward" emblazoned across it. The Third Ward, which you'll be hiking through for the next hour or so, was a wholesale and manufacturing district at the turn of the century. Many of its buildings have been restored and are used for everything from produce distribution to theaters.

Turn right at the first street north of the river, Erie, and walk east. The first building on the left is notable for a couple of reasons. It was constructed in 1904 as the Pabst Brewing Company Saloon and Boardinghouse, and it is built of Cream City brick. This brick, used in many of Milwaukee's older buildings, has a fascinating history. According to John G. Gregory, in his *History of Milwaukee, Wisconsin* (1931), "There was disappointment at first at the color of the bricks, when it was found that the heat of the kiln turned the clay to a pale yellow instead of red, as is the case of bricks produced elsewhere. When travelers praised the cheerful appearance of structures made of Milwaukee brick, the townsfolk not only became reconciled, but learned to regard the distinctive color with local pride."

Farther east on Erie is the Milwaukee Terminal Building, which now houses the Milwaukee Institute of Art and Design. The garage-size sculptures along the street make the building's current purpose unmistakable.

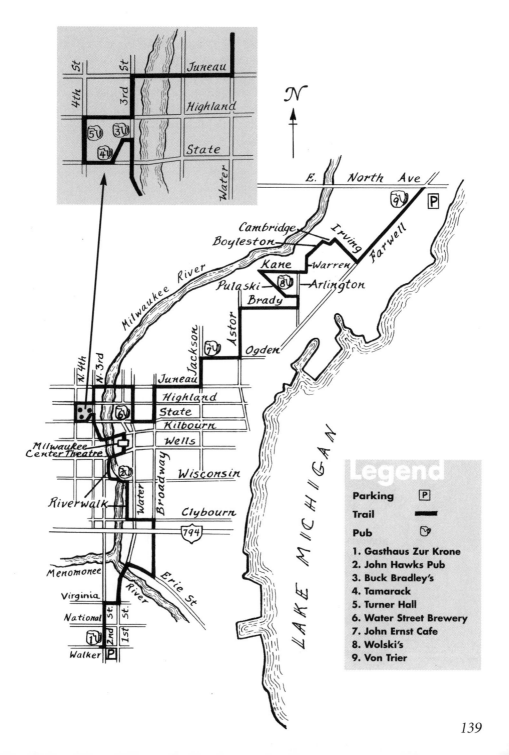

Legend

Parking	P
Trail	▬
Pub	🍺

1. Gasthaus Zur Krone
2. John Hawks Pub
3. Buck Bradley's
4. Tamarack
5. Turner Hall
6. Water Street Brewery
7. John Ernst Cafe
8. Wolski's
9. Von Trier

Just past the east end of the Terminal Building, make a left turn onto Broadway. There's an outstanding little cafe—Cafe Marche—on the corner and a little city park to the east. The next three blocks along Broadway are full of historic and interesting buildings. At 158 N. Broadway is the World Performance Exchange, an amalgamation of several theaters. Just north of the theaters is Engine Company #10 Firehouse. Originally built in 1893, it carries the dubious distinction of being the only firehouse in Milwaukee's history destroyed by fire. On the northwest corner of Buffalo and Broadway, a long, narrow building that dates from 1894 houses wholesale grocery and produce operations, and has for almost a hundred years.

Your exit from the Historic Third Ward is heralded by the massive eight lanes of I-794 passing overhead. Turn left on Clybourn and walk one block west to Water Street. Turn right without crossing the Milwaukee River and you'll be headed north on the River Walk along Water Street. By now you're undoubtedly thirsty so amble quickly past the Gimbel's Building (the east end of the Grand Avenue mall), which sits on the west side of the river along Wisconsin Avenue. Cross Wisconsin Avenue and you're at the entrance to John Hawks Pub, located in the 100 East Building, on the site of one of Milwaukee's first skyscrapers—the 14-story Pabst Building, built in 1892.

John Hawks Pub has an outdoor terrace perched over the Milwaukee River. It's named after a 14th-century English soldier of fortune who fought in enough battles to drive anyone to drink. The food is good, the urban scenery stimulating, and, if the weather's nice, you may be tempted to end your tour here. Resist. There's lots more to come.

Exit John Hawks Pub on Wisconsin Avenue (where you entered), and cross the river. Turn right and follow the River Walk north to Wells Street. At Wells Street, jog back east across the river and walk past the building on the northeast corner of the River Walk and Wells Street, which was constructed in 1898 by the Milwaukee Electric Railway & Light Company. Refurbished in 1989, it now serves as the Milwaukee Center Theater. Enter the complex off of Wells Street. As you stroll through this lovely corridor, which links four theaters and the Wyndham Hotel, note the Pabst Theater off to your right. One of Milwaukee's architectural and cultural jewels, the Pabst Theater was built by Jacob Nunnemacher in 1871 as an opera house and German cafe. A fire in 1895 destroyed most of the building, which was then owned by Frederick Pabst. Pabst had it rebuilt within six months. Restored in 1976, the theater seats almost 1,400 people.

Exiting the theater complex onto Kilbourn Street, you'll see the massive Performing Arts Center (P.A.C.) across the street. Uihlein Hall, located within the P.A.C., seats 2,300 people! Turn left on Kilbourn, and cross the river once more. On the other side turn right (north) through Pere Marquette Park to North 3rd Street. When you cross State Street, you will enter what's called "Old World Third Street."

There are three notable taverns here. The first is Buck Bradley's, at 1019 3rd St. According to a history printed on the tavern's menu, this is one of the oldest buildings in Milwaukee. It started out in 1854 as the Pioneer Furniture Store. Renovated in the early 1990s, the tavern now claims "the largest bar in the state of Wisconsin." Made out of cherry wood, there's no doubt about its beauty.

Go out the back door of Buck Bradley's, turn left (south) down the alley, and you'll find the Tamarack (322 W. State St.), which, according to its menu, is "one of the oldest watering holes in the city." The building was built as a tavern by the Schlitz brewery in 1889. It's said that the typewriter was developed on the site in 1869, by a Milwaukeean named Christian Latham Sholes.

From the Tamarack, turn right on State Street, then right again on 4th Street, till you come to the Historic Turner Restaurant. The building, properly called Turner Hall, was constructed in 1883. It was built by a German association called the Sozialer Turnverein, which believed in physical fitness. Hence, the building houses a gymnasium. Another "gymnasium," a bit more modern, sits across 4th Street from Turner Hall: the Bradley Center, home to Milwaukee's professional basketball and hockey teams. The eight-sided building was built in 1988 as a gift to the community from Jane Pettit, the daughter of industrialist Harry Lynde Bradley, whose octagonal-faced factory clock shadowed the beginning of this walk.

From Turner Hall, continue north on 4th Street to Highland, then turn right and walk to 3rd Street. If you look south, to your right, on 3rd, you'll see Usingers, Mader's Restaurant, the Spice House and the Ambrosia Chocolate store. Check them out if you'd like, then head north on 3rd one block to Juneau Avenue. Turn right and cross the Milwaukee River one last time. When you reach the middle of the bridge, look down the river, between two downtown buildings. You can see the Allen-Bradley clock tower. That's two blocks from where we started this walk! Just to the right of the buildings through which you are viewing the clock tower, a copper dome with an American flag sits atop Milwaukee City Hall. The city hall was built in 1895, and its 350-foot-high tower made it the third tallest building in the country at that time. Look west down Juneau Avenue and you can see the hulking Pabst Brewery Malt Elevator, a behemoth of a building that stands 184 feet tall. It holds 840,000 bushels of malt and related brewing products.

As you continue across the bridge, note the boats, docks and low buildings just to your right on the east shore. These modern structures are the River Houses Condominiums. They were built in 1985 and offer 1,500 square feet of downtown residential living space, complete with personal marina.

Continue walking down Juneau Avenue to the second cross street, which will be Water Street. Turn right onto Water and at the corner of Water and State streets you'll find the Water Street Brewery, one of Milwaukee's few brew pubs. While the architecture is dance-club modern, the home-brewed beer is worth a try. So is the food. For barbecue fans, Brew City BBQ across Water Street offers great sauces.

When you leave the Water Street Brewery, head east down State Street to North Broadway. Turn left (north) on Broadway and walk to Juneau Avenue. Turn right (east) on Juneau Avenue and walk to North Jackson Street, where you'll turn left (north).

The John Ernst Cafe is located on the northeast corner of the intersection of Jackson Street and East Ogden. Stop in. John and Jim Lindenberg are third-generation owners. According to John, the cafe is the oldest restaurant in Milwaukee, dating back to 1878, when it was called Mother Heiser's Ogden Cafe.

Out the door of the John Ernst Cafe, turn left (east) on Ogden, and you'll walk along block after block of brick apartment buildings. Although they look older, all were built in the 1980s. This entire stretch of neighborhood, to Astor Street and beyond, was demolished in the 1960s to make way for the eastern extension of the Park Freeway. Local resistance stalled, and eventually prevented, the completion of the freeway. Some unusual trees are planted on the parkway between the sidewalk and Ogden. The city is experimenting with bald cypress, a deciduous (meaning it drops its leaves in fall) conifer, like our native tamarack. The tree's fine-textured needles and pyramidal shape make it a nifty-looking street tree.

Once you reach the intersection of Ogden and Astor, look at the church on the southeast corner. It's the First Unitarian Church of Milwaukee. The congregation was founded in 1842.

Turn left (north) on Astor Street, and when you cross the next street—Lyon—you'll notice you've crossed into an older residential neighborhood. You'll pass Mt. Zion Church of God in Christ and then Eddie Glorioso's Market. Then you'll reach Brady Street, Milwaukee's answer to Haight-Ashbury. Actually, Brady Street combines ethnicity with eccentricity in a truly unique way.

Turn right (east) on Brady. Bon Appetit Restaurant on the left, a block east of Astor, is famous for Mediterranean food. Another Glorioso's food store sits on the north side of the street. It's owned by Eddie's brother. You'll walk under the sign for Art Smart's Dart Mart and Juggling Emporium and past Peter Sciortino's Bakery before you turn left onto Arlington. Turn left again at the first crossroad, North Pulaski, and continue past the Peter Weiland & Co. organ builders shop. You'll see Wolski's on the right. The place is small. It has wood floors and a wood ceiling. It smells like a bar. According to 23-year owner Mike Bondar, Wolski's is the 13th-oldest licensed bar in Milwaukee. Head to the back of the building and you'll see a panorama of dart boards, and a collection of plaques to go with them, testifying to the excellent aim of the bar's dart team. And try the pretzels, they're good.

Continue northwest on Pulaski, then turn right on Kane. The area along Kane was a blue-collar community back in the early 1990s, when Milwaukee's factories and foundries and breweries really hummed with business. Run-down and neglected through the middle of the century, the neighborhood is reborn, with many of the old structures cleaned up and remodeled.

Follow the series of short blocks along the park on your left, which is called Caesar's Park. Take Warren to Boyleston to Cambridge to Irving. Turn right on Irving and walk east until you reach Farwell, and then turn left. Farwell is noted for being one of the first commercial centers on the north side. You'll pass the old Oriental Theater. Built in 1927, it's one of the last old movie theaters left in Milwaukee. It originally seated 2,500 people! The ornate lobby has been restored.

Your last stop is at Von Trier, 2235 N. Farwell, at Farwell's intersection with North Avenue. With an outdoor beer garden and heavy German decoration inside, it seems a fitting place to quaff one of more than 70 kinds of beer offered and relax after a five-mile tour of some of the oldest and most interesting buildings in Wisconsin. Maybe you should try some Steinhaeger with your beer. This German gin is said to be good for sore feet! ▲

42

Riverfront and Stagecoach Segments of the Green Circle Trail
City of Stevens Point

Amble alongside the Wisconsin River on a
bucolic trail designed for city dwellers.

Distance: Seven miles round trip.

Time: Three to four hours round trip.

Path: A flat path, marked with "Green Circle" signs and wood signs that denote on which of the trail's 12 segments you're walking.

Directions: Park anywhere downtown in Stevens Point and walk to the Highway 10 bridge over the Wisconsin River. The trail crosses Highway 10 just east of the river.

Contact: Stevens Point Area Chamber of Commerce
600 Main St., Stevens Point, WI 54481; (715) 344-1940.

The first half of this walk is along the Wisconsin River through exemplary city parks, full of trees and open spaces. One park has a beach. The second half of the route is a mile-long walk through a stretch of partially wooded, roadless terrain.

Start where the Green Circle Trail crosses Highway 10 and goes north. On a warm summer's day the hum of a bank's air conditioner reminds you that this is an urban walk. Next to the bank is the Chamber of Commerce building. If you need a map or other information about the area, this is the place to stop.

The paved path leads you to a kiosk, which describes the 24-mile-long Green Circle Trail project and identifies some people and businesses that have contributed funds. The purpose of the trail is to provide "natural areas" at the doorstep of city dwellers. The path traces a rough circle from the north side of Stevens Point to the village of Whiting on the south. It's bounded on the west by the Wisconsin River and, on the east, by the Plover River. Another kiosk describes the Stevens Point Area Foundation's Memorial Tree Planting. More than a hundred trees, all planted in memory of someone, line the walkway

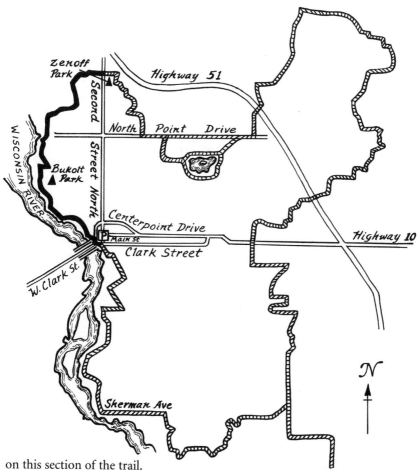

Legend

Parking ▣

Trail ▬

Intersecting
Trail ▨

on this section of the trail.

The view of the river here is excellent, as it is from many places along this walk. A look back south, down the river, gives a good view of the Highway 10 bridge, the big Stevens Point water tower and the Consolidated Papers mill.

Continue up the trail and you'll pass a boat launching site and some moored boats. The river here can be busy on a summer weekend, but most weekdays are without boat traffic.

About a half-mile into the walk, you'll pass two trees on the left, growing on the riverbank. These box-elder are notable for their prostrate position. Both fell back onto the grass 20 or so years ago but didn't die. Instead, they continued to grow, branches climbing upward from horizontal trunks. Some of the branches reach 30 feet into the air.

Just before you reach Fourth Avenue, the path briefly enters a canopy of trees. Their diversity is worth note. There are alder, elm, ash, mountain ash, cherry, sumac, box-elder, spruce and black locust, all within a few feet of one another along the trail. You'll see black locust several more times down the trail.

When you pass a second boat launch, you will be entering bucolic Bukolt Park. A landscape planting of shrub roses marks the formal entrance to the park, and if they are in bloom, you may smell them before you see them. In addition to a swimming beach, Bukolt offers toilets and a pop machine. Ducks, and sometimes geese, paddle and waddle through the park. There are two roadways through the park. Take the one closest to the river and you'll be on a peninsula between a pond and the river. This route affords the best view.

The segment of trail north of the park is called Stagecoach. You'll walk on or near roadways for about a quarter mile and then past St. Peter Cemetery, which is located on the banks of the river. Most of the trail has been sited just off the road, along boardwalks and paths in the woods.

Just after crossing North Point Drive, the trail veers right and away from all roads for the next mile or so. Here it's called the Larry Fritsch Pathway. After a brief walk through a stand of jack pine, you'll enter a pure stand of black locust. These fine-leafed trees form a gossamerlike canopy of leaves high overhead. Their gently arching, rarely straight trunks etch dark lines against the filtered skylight. And if you're lucky enough to walk here in mid-June, the fragrance from the dense panicles of white blossoms will complete the sensual picture.

Emerging from the locust, you'll enter a large, 20-acre oak opening, probably an old farmfield. Scattered Hill's oak and jack pine punctuate an austere, dry landscape. Sand blows, areas of pure-white sand, stand out against the green. Petals of pink wild roses peek above the grasses, and hawkweed nods in the breeze. The contrast between forest and prairie is sharp.

The next woods you enter is primarily birch and aspen, white and gray-green trunks shining in the shade. The trail here can be wet, but much work has been done hauling bark to raise the grade. The ground stays wet as you enter another woodland type, an extremely dense stand of white pine. Bridges and walkways have been built over the wettest parts of the trail.

A couple hundred yards after exiting the pine woods, you'll reach North Second Street and Zenoff Park, a major softball complex. This is your turn-around point. Retrace your steps to return to your car. ▲

Snowy Adventures

43

Blackjack Springs
Wilderness Area
Nicolet National Forest

*Look for deer tracks, grouse, open springs and
one of the state's largest expanses of big pine trees
on a snowshoe walk to a remote canyon.*

Distance: About five miles.

Time: Three to five hours.

Path: There is no path. This is an unmarked walk to be done on snow-shoes. A compass is essential. The terrain is an open, rolling woods with a fairly steep descent to Blackjack Springs.

Directions: From the intersection of Highway 45 and Highway 70 just east of Eagle River, take Highway 70 east 6.5 miles to Forest Road 2178. Turn left and take FR 2178 for 6.25 miles to a parking area on the right side of the road. (If you cross the Deerskin River, you went .1 mile too far.)

Contact: Nicolet National Forest, Eagle River Ranger Station
P.O. Box 1809, 4364 Wall St., Eagle River, WI 54521; (715) 479-2827, TDD (715) 479-1308.

Blackjack Springs Wilderness Area was logged in the early 1900s but it still contains a large expanse of big white and red pine. On the first part of the walk, the splashing and gurgling of the Deerskin River is delightful. The feel of the area around Blackjack Springs is remote and very Western, with more large trees and a deep canyon.

Dive into the woods across the road from the parking area west of FR 2178 and just south of the Deerskin River. There's a high bank along the road here, and in deep snow it's a difficult beginning. Don't give up; things get much easier once you're in the woods.

The river will be your guide on the first part of this walk, so keep it within sight or hearing. You will be on its south side. The topography along the shore is quite similar the entire way to Blackjack Creek. It consists of three tiers. There's the actual river floodplain, in some places no wider than the river itself and in others several hundred yards wide and covered with alder. Then there's a plateau that's a few feet higher than the floodplain, essentially flat and varying in width from almost nonexistent in a few places to several hundred yards wide. Finally, there's a slope, sometimes at a steep 55-degree angle, which takes you to the gently undulating upland.

The river itself is the northern boundary of the wilderness area. It is narrow and usually open, except in the dead of winter when air temperatures are consistently around and below zero. Stop and watch the water for a while; look into one of the deeper pools. You may see some fish, little minnows or bigger smallmouth bass.

This walk continues along the Deerskin River, which gradually turns to the south through a mixed, mostly conifer woods. Seeing jack pine, which normally loves dry soil, and balsam fir, which loves moist soil, growing side by side is unusual, but it happens here. About 15 minutes into the walk you'll snowshoe through another uncommon forest association: a pure stand of black spruce, growing up on the plateau between the river and the slope to the uplands. It's unusual to find a pure stand of these trees, and even more unusual to find them on such a dry site; usually black spruce grow in bogs. It is likely that the water table here is very high, and the black spruce roots access it early in their growth.

About a half-mile into the walk, you will encounter an area where the slope to the uplands retreats far to the south. The Deerskin turns back west here. In order to follow it, you will walk down off the plateau and enter a bog populated by black spruce, tamarack and a few alder. Walking up a big hill on the other side, you will pass some large white pine; they stand more than a hundred feet tall on the crest of the hill. This hilltop continues for a few hundred feet, then slowly slopes down to an old logging road. Stay close to the river and you will see a footbridge. The bridge is narrow, and when the snow is deep, looks like an overly long piece of cake with white icing piled too high.

Do not cross the bridge, but instead go south on the old logging road. Note the trees that have been planted in the road. These white pine were put here to discourage motorized travel. The road loops gently back to the east as it climbs up from the river. There are more lovely big old white pine near the road's summit. At the summit, 1,712 feet above sea level and the highest ground attained on this walk, you will note that the woods change. To the east, the big conifers are gone, and smaller birch and aspen predominate. To the west there are more conifers of size. We want to take a right turn near the summit and head southwest. There is an unmarked but quite visible road here.

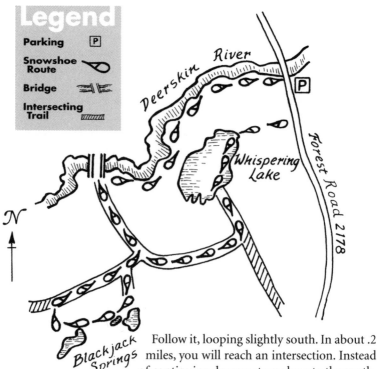

Follow it, looping slightly south. In about .2 miles, you will reach an intersection. Instead of continuing down a steep slope to the south, bear right and follow the road as it traces the lip of the slope, heading generally west.

The woods here consists of one of the largest expanses of big white and red pine anywhere in the state. Note the thickness of the trunks and the tallness of the trees. To the south, down the slope and one ridge beyond are the Blackjack Springs, the object of this walk. Follow the road another .2 miles to where it leaves the lip of the slope. Then turn left off the road and head south and a bit east (compass heading: 170 degrees). The walking will be rough for a bit, with downed trees and some brush. You may need to go up and down one or two ravines before you spy the springs. If you don't see the springs, or at least a creek bottom, turn farther east, about 120 degrees, and proceed.

In winters of deep snow, you'll see signs of deer (tracks, scat and browse marks) near the springs. Deer are attracted to the area's open water, cedar and other dense conifers. Grouse like it here, too, so don't be too surprised if one bursts from beneath the snow.

The springs form a series of small ponds, connected by an intermittent creek. They remain at least partially open in all but the coldest weather. Be extremely careful if you decide to venture out onto them. The warm water seeping from below thins the ice from the bottom up, sometimes hiding unsafe conditions.

Once you reach the springs, turn left and follow along the hillside (much easier than walking the spring's edge). You'll be heading east northeast. When the springs end, turn a bit more north and continue on. You will either cross your own trail, snowshoe prints clear in the snow, or you will come upon the pine-planted road, hitting it somewhere past where you turned off to go to the springs. Turn right and follow that road until it intersects a marked path, in about .4 mile. Take the path left and in another .3 mile you will see Whispering Lake in front of you. Traverse the lake or the lakeshore on its east side up to its north end, then head east as you leave the lake. In about .2 mile you will cross FR 2178. The parking area will be to your left, about .3 mile away. ▲

44

Mink River Estuary
Nature Conservancy Preserve

Explore a cedar forest and a
frozen creek on a challenging snowshoe
hike through a nature sanctuary.

Distance: About six miles.

Time: Four to five hours.

Path: This is the toughest hike in this book. Most of the time, there is no path, though you will follow a snowmobile trail part of the way. The terrain is generally flat except for the slope between the upland and lowland forest types. However, fallen trees and a thick understory can make walking extremely difficult. The deeper the snow, the more difficult the walk. Snowshoes are recommended, and a compass is essential.

Directions: From the intersection of Highway 42 and County ZZ in Sister Bay, follow County ZZ east approximately four miles to Mink River Road and drive one mile to a parking area on the right. Note: The parking area may not be plowed.

Contact: The Nature Conservancy
633 W. Main St., Madison, WI 53703; (608) 251-8140.

The Mink River is short—less than three miles from its spring-fed headwaters to Rowley Bay and the vastness of Lake Michigan beyond. Along these three miles the river's slight current encounters "seiches," wavelike, regular oscillations of the water level originating in the lake. Much like a tide, these oscillations mix the strongly alkaline spring water that runs the river with lake water, creating an estuary. This habitat is extremely sensitive and ecologically important, providing a sanctuary for waterfowl, spawning grounds for fish and a critical stopover for migrating birds. According to *The Places We Save*, a Nature Conservancy publication, the Mink River Estuary is one of the few high-quality estuaries remaining in this country.

Much of the estuary's hundreds of acres of cedar forest are wet, too wet to comfortably walk through in spring, summer and fall. But in winter, it's snow-covered and, for the most part, frozen, giving walkers a unique opportunity. You can experience the place not only from the river, as canoeists do in other seasons, but you can explore the shore and inland areas. The open marsh surrounding the river, the alder thickets and the tamarack bogs are all accessible to you. Plus, a winter walker can cross the river at will (always being careful, of course) and explore both sides. Obviously, parts of this walk won't be possible unless things have frozen up well. Make decisions accordingly.

This walk begins from the parking area east of Mink River Road. An enclosed Nature Conservancy signboard is located there and provides information about the area. No maps or other take-along information is available. Trying to follow the trail that leads east from the information board will not work. It's not a winter trail and whatever makes it obvious to walkers when there isn't snow on the ground can't be seen when the trail's covered with white. So get out your compass.

Head due east. You'll walk through a mixture of trees, and soon note a gradual slope taking you down into more heavily evergreened woods. Within five minutes of starting your walk you should reach a "creek," which doesn't show up on any of the conservancy maps. It's only a few feet wide and, oddly, flows north. Turn left and follow it downstream. If you're lucky, you'll find a small, 4-foot by 8-foot pool created by a downed log. This crystal-clear, ice-cold window lets you see the intricacy below. Twigs and needles, some still green, greet your eyes. It's an elaborate picture, painted by trees dropping parts of themselves into the playful water, and framed by bright white snow.

As you continue north, the wind-thrown trees will begin annoying you. These trees, cedar and aspen, have been toppled by the west wind, and therefore lay across your route. Somewhere in this wild tangle the "creek" disappears, replaced by occasional pothole springs, some open, some with a skin of ice over them. This area would be entirely unpleasant if insufficiently frozen. If you do begin having a problem with too much water, head back west and you will find the upland woods not far away.

Whether you persevere down in the swamp or up in the highland, continue north and you will come to a raised grade—some kind of narrow roadbed. (If you have had enough walking already, turn left and head west out to the Mink River Road. It's about .3 mile away. From there, you can reach the spot where you began this walk by turning left and walking down the road about a quarter mile.) To continue this walk, turn right and head east. Stop somewhere along the grade and look into the woods. It's a jumble, full of texture—tree trunks standing upright mixed with trees canted at all angles by wind and soggy footing. Let the colors seep in, the tan-tinged green of cedar, the darker green of balsam fir and the occasional stark yellow-green of a dying balsam fir, all of it punctuated by blood-red dogwood twigs.

It's about .3 mile to a snowmobile trail. Take the snowmobile trail south. It cuts through smaller upland hardwoods. In about a quarter mile, a trail heads off to the left toward the Mink River. Take that trail and you will soon be headed downhill and into a lowland forest, full of cedar again.

Just before you reach the river, the conifers will all but disappear. You may see the giant sugar maple on your left; it's more than 3 feet in diameter and probably more than a hundred feet tall.

If it's a sunny day, or even if it's mildly overcast, get ready to squint. The brightness as you exit the woods is blinding. The river bed is surprisingly broad (600 feet or so) and shaped like a bow here. Look to the right and you can see the river's mouth, about half a mile downstream.

For now, walk upriver, following the snowmobile trail. You'll round a point of land and see the entire 1.5-mile length of the river that lies north of you. It looks like a long way, but don't worry; you're not going that far. You're heading for the snowmobile trail across the river, marked by two orange reflective markers. Follow it on shore past another Nature Conservancy signboard. Continue on the snowmobile trail. It winds through lowlands and then climbs that ubiquitous slope to the upland. It's a little over a mile to a trailhead at a bend in County NP.

From here, dive back into the woods, and, using your compass for guidance, head due west. Even though it's not marked, you'll be following the Nature Conservancy boundary. Your goal again is the river. At first you will walk through upland forest, easy going. Then you'll enter the lowland forest and begin to see more and more big cedar. Still easy going. Then you'll come upon "The Tangle." Although it's only about .2 mile to the river, this is a tough stretch. Trees have fallen in all directions. Some of the cedars are large and held up off the ground by their dense branches and massive roots. Even limbless trunks are three feet off the ground and hard to step over. More insidious are the low-lying trunks and limbs, buried by snow and waiting to catch the tips of your snowshoes. Use small trees and branches as handholds as you maneuver over and through the mess. The Tangle has one redeeming feature: It offers many excellent places to sit and rest or have lunch.

When you come to the edge of the trees, there's still more travail ahead. The next few hundred yards is guarded by alder. They thin out

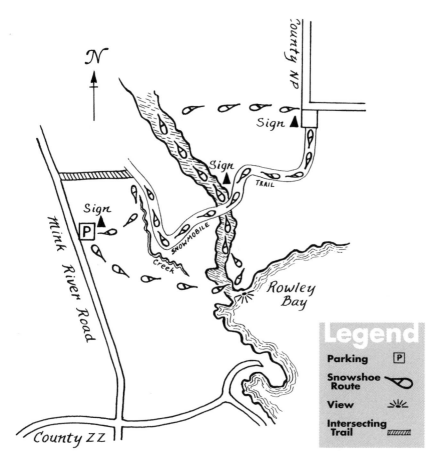

as you approach a marsh, but, as always, an alder thicket is a real "in-your-face" experience. Note that new types of vegetation appear. There's a jointed grass and some type of plume grass that stands more than 6 feet tall, its pyramid-shaped plume dangling from a long, slender stalk.

One more obstacle awaits. The wind sweeps a lot of snow across the river opening and deposits it amid the marsh plants you have to cross before reaching the river. So take a deep breath before striding ahead. If you're tired, cut to the river in as direct a fashion as possible so you can walk on it instead of through the marsh. If the river isn't safe right there, head south along the edge of the marsh toward a point occupied by a single, bushy cedar tree, about .3 mile away. Note that west, across the river, two houses are visible. (That area is not part of conservancy land.)

From the cedar tree, continue your walk south on the river. You'll come back to the snowmobile trail. Follow it down the river, past where you've been before (you'll see the signboard on your left) to the spot where your trail exits from the west shore. Don't take that path back into the woods but instead head southeast across the river into the shrubby shoreline alders, past a few more windthrown trees and into the woods. Your objective is Rowley Bay. Your reward when you arrive at the bay is an expansive view of ice and deep-blue water, with tall pressure ridges between.

To your right, a small point of land guards the mouth of the river. Walk to it. A compass bearing of 275 degrees (5 degrees north of west) will take you back to the parking area. It's about 1.2 miles. ▲

45

Squaw Bay Sea Caves
Apostle Islands
National Lakeshore

*Brave a trek on frozen Lake Superior
to see spectacular ice formations.*

Distance: Five miles round trip.

Time: Three to six hours.

Path: You will be walking on frozen Lake Superior. Unless you arrive shortly after a snowfall or major wind, an unmarked but well-worn, snow-packed trail winds out across Squaw Bay. Be aware, however, that this big lake does not freeze as a pristine ice sheet. Hunks of ice are blown into the bay in late fall and early winter, forming pack ice that eventually congeals into the hard surface tramped by sightseers. This process creates an uneven, lump-filled ice; expect to negotiate a slippery, protrusion-filled path. Unless you arrive after a significant snowfall, snowshoes will be more troublesome than helpful. Wear warm boots that provide good traction. Ice crampons would be OK, but aren't necessary since the terrain is flat.

Directions: From Bayfield, take Highway 13 north and west 17.75 miles to Meyers Road. Meyers Road is not signed. It only goes right off of Highway 13, and takes you one-half mile to a small parking area on top of a low bluff overlooking Lake Superior. Wooden steps lead down to the shore.

Contact: Apostle Islands National Lakeshore
Route 1, Box 4, Bayfield, WI 54814; (715) 779-3397.

Lake Superior is a highlight of this walk. In middle and late winter, which is the only time you can take this walk, the lake lies motionless. It's not entirely silent, though, because the ice that embraces the cold water below it sometimes resounds with a crack, like the report of a rifle. Water, unlike any other fluid on Earth or anywhere as far as we know, expands as it cools and must make room for its freezing self. It makes noise in the process.

The wind can be a highlight, too. Be ready for it. Windchill has meaning here. Yet if you expect buffeting and dress well, there's triumph to be won crossing the open expanse of bay. The howling wind just adds to the exhilaration, fills you up more, blows a better story.

The object of our walk is a view of modest "sea caves" that wave action, over the last few thousand years, has carved into cliffs that rise 50 to 80 feet above the lake's surface. Before it froze, Lake Superior threw itself against the shore. This spray, plus the seepage of water off the land and down the bluffs, freezes and creates ice sculptures amid the sea caves.

Descend the steps at the end of Meyers Road onto the snow and ice-covered beach. Looking northeast from the base of the wooden steps, you can see the cliffs about a mile away. You're headed out across the bay to the farthest point of land.

There's often an ice ridge near shore that may be more than 6 feet high. Walk along the beach and search for an easy entrance to the lake, or clamber carefully over the ridge.

As you near the cliffs, you'll notice odd-looking, variously colored lumps clinging to them. These are aggregations of ice, formed in three ways. In one process, mist and spray, rising from the lake's surface before it froze, encrusted the trees and shrubs on the cliff with milky-white ice. In another process, ice formed as snow above the cliff melted and seeped down onto the cliff face. This is colored by the soil that seeped with it, and appears in shades of brown, green and yellow. In a third process, water originated from springs between the sandstone layers that compose the cliff and then froze. This water is intensely blue—glacier blue.

Round the point that has been your destination and you will see a series of small points extending farther along the shore that jut out into the lake. Each encloses a cove and each cove harbors surprise. One of the first is a deep gorge that cuts a V-shaped notch about a hundred feet into the cliff. Inside, stalactitelike icicles hang from on high, and a waterfall cascades silently down one side. As the cliff closes above you at the back of the V, white birch trees stretch up to the sky, adding depth and perspective to a sliver of sky. Remind yourself that you stand atop water, deep water, water that in summer would be over your head.

Not far from the gorge is the "circle cave." Enter the broad opening, and you'll find a cave that is essentially round, especially the ceiling. Look up and notice the layers of sandstone worn into concentric rings by ferocious whirlpools spun by giant waves. Take a deep breath and imagine being underwater here, twirled and dashed around as if you were nothing.

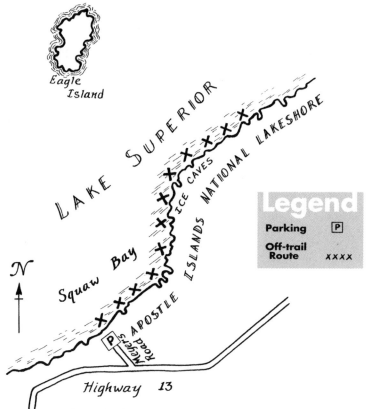

Along the base of the cliff, seeps, springs and spray sometimes create a massive wall of ice. Small caves lie hidden under and behind this ice. Brave explorers prostrate themselves before this ice wall and crawl into such caves. The ceilings are covered with crystalline ice formations, more delicate and finer in detail than the exterior ice.

The next cove beyond the circle cave is the largest cove on this walk. Its pleasant, gentle sweep accentuates the colorful array of natural ice sculptures hugging the cliff.

Two outstanding rock pedestals mark the end of the outbound walk. These pillars of sandstone support the cliff above and create a natural arch under which you can walk with plenty of head room. The shoreline stretches away beyond these arches to the northeast, and the cliffs shorten, becoming less than 20 feet high.

The walk back is straightforward. Simply turn around and retrace your steps. If you want variation, try staying close to the cliffs until you can walk on the beach rather than crossing Squaw Bay.

Snowmobiles take this route so there is usually a path, sometimes less jumbled than the one out on the ice.

A few words about safety seem warranted. The pamphlet published by the Department of the Interior on the Squaw Bay Sea Caves devotes more than 20 percent of its copy to "Safety." Some winter advice includes, "Beware of cracks in the ice even on the coldest days. It is advisable to carry an ice bar to test ice thickness. Watch out for falling ice in and around cliffs and caves. Falling rock is also a potential hazard."

Don't be intimidated, but do be careful. Check with the folks at park headquarters and if there's any doubt about safety, don't venture out. Water is fluid, and so are conditions. ▲

MORE BOOKS
ON WISCONSIN
FROM WISCONSIN TRAILS

The Wisconsin Traveler's Companion
A Guide to Country Sights
by Jerry Apps and Julie Sutter-Blair

County Parks of Wisconsin
by Jeannette and Chet Bell

Great Weekend Adventures
from the Editors of Wisconsin Trails

Best Wisconsin Bike Trips
by Phil Van Valkenberg

Best Canoe Trails of Southern Wisconsin
by Michael E. Duncanson

Great Golf in Wisconsin
by John Hughes and Jeff Mayers

Wisconsin, The Story of the Badger State
by Norman K. Risjord

Barns of Wisconsin
by Jerry Apps

Mills of Wisconsin
by Jerry Apps and Allen Strang

Wisconsin Trails
P.O. Box 5650
Madison, WI 53705
(800) 236-8088